Alan Coren's Sunday Best

Illustrations by Gray Jolliffe

Published in association with
the *Sunday Express*

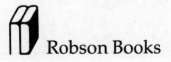

Robson Books

Alan Coren and Robson Books would like to thank the editor and staff of the *Sunday Express*, in which this material first appeared, for all their unstinting advice and co-operation.

First published in Great Britain in 1993
by Robson Books Ltd, Bolsover House,
5–6 Clipstone Street, London W1P 7EB

**British Library Cataloguing in Publication
Data**
A catalogue record for this title is available from
the British Library

ISBN 0 86051 870 1

Designed by Harold King
Set in Times by
Columns Design & Production Services Ltd.
Reading
Printed by Butler & Tanner, Frome and London

The History of Jobbing Britain

Since 1 February traditionally marks the opening of the DIY season, what better moment could there be to make ourselves a handy wall chart tracing the development of the tradition itself? Here is one I cobbled together earlier:

55 BC Caesar's first expedition enjoys unopposed landing, after: (a) hub bolts shear on British troop carts, leaving army miles from coast attempting to whittle new axles, hampered by fact that all knives are in for annual sharpening and not due back for six months on account of staff holidays, lack of whetstones, wrong type of frost in Weald, etc; (b) main British deterrent (Big Stick With Nail In, Mark III) fails, as the result of all nails hammered in bent, big sticks split at knot hole, string handles unwind, name tapes fall off; (c) British commander-in-chief accidentally killed putting up shelf in kitchen.

AD 61 First British uprising. DIY enthusiast Boadicea of the Iceni hits on plan of affixing sword blades to chariot wheels. Thumbless Iceni cavalry goes into action, sword blades fall off, uprising fails.

122 Britons finally concede Roman superiority after Hadrian builds wall from Tyne to Solway. Biggest British-built wall up until then was four feet long and collapsed under sleet. Roman hegemony now totally unopposed, since

many Britons believe Romans to be gods.

410 After four centuries of training local labour, Romans still find forts fall over when door slams, galleys submerge on launching, siege engines drop boulders on crews, and 80 per cent of local labour now either crippled or nailed to one another. Romans pack up and leave.

600 Successful invasions by Angles, Saxons and Jutes, since:
(a) two centuries of Roman absence have left Britain with no roads (all attempts to repair them having resulted in workers shovelling toes off) and defending army consequently drowns in potholes on way to coast;
(b) main British deterrent (Big Stick With Nail In Mark MCMXLVI) fails after discovery that all nails in bargain job lot have heads at both ends;
(c) British commander-in-chief accidentally killed putting up hat peg in hall.

643 Christianity finally comes to Britain when, after two centuries of struggle against appalling odds, British carpenters manage to make a cross. Night of revelry follows, with beacons on every hill. Cross

falls over. Hills burn down.

794 After six generations of savage internal warring between Mercia, Wessex, Northumbria, East Anglia, Kent and Sussex (any attempt at peace treaties having been thwarted by drawing-pins popping out, maps suddenly rolling up and knocking beer over, map tables collapsing, wax dripping off candles and setting light to conference hut, tent poles snapping and falling on delegates, peace offerings coming unglued as soon as delegates get home, etc), Britain in no position to resist Danish invasion. Danes settle.

876 Alfred and his brother King Burgred of Mercia join forces to rise up against the Danes in the south. Using time-honoured British navigational methods, home-made compasses and charts, and their intimate knowledge of the terrain, Burgred's army walks into the sea, Alfred's army discovers Glasgow, and Alfred himself ends up in an old Welshwoman's hut, where he burns the cakes.

877 Alfred burns the oven.

878 Alfred burns the hut.

879 After Alfred burns

the cow, old woman's husband finally throws him out, king or no king.

886 Alfred takes London, but only after Danes move out. Danes sick of banging heads on low beams, falling through rotted floorboards, not being able to open wonky doors, also constantly getting wedged in narrow alleys, plus Londoners throwing rubbish out of windows on to them (no internal plumbing, since principle of hollow pipe beyond English grasp).

1016 Danes invade again, and Cnut becomes king. Not universally loved (many references to 'Silly Cnut' scrawled on walls by British scholars) until hits on plan to personally reverse sea, commending him to British DIY enthusiasts everywhere. Plan fails, though watching Britons unable to understand why. General opinion is that Cnut using wrong glue, or possibly sea contains manufacturer's design fault.

1066 Normans invade. Harold shoots self in eye with home-made bow.

1070 Domesday Book commissioned. Severe editorial problems, since by second edition almost everything listed in first

Remember how tedious this was before we invented power tools?

edition has fallen down. Normans decide to build own things, just to fill up book, and introduce English Perpendicular, based on improvements to English Leaning and English Horizontal. Britons amazed to find churches taller than they are.

1215 Sick of King John not doing anything, barons decide to do it themselves. Magna Carta signed.

1216 Magna Carta invalidated by John on grounds that barons did not tear off guarantee on facing page and post within 14 days. Civil war. John's army defeated since armoured elbows hinged wrong way and infantry beat itself to death in first engagement.

1314 Bannockburn. In 1313, Robert the Bruce, sickened by his inability to paper spare room, is inspired by spider to try again. He does so, and ceiling falls on him. After that, in quick succession, puts scaffold board through window, paints self into corner, screws cat to skirting, knocks banisters out with his steps, and plasters over back door. Eventually becomes so enraged with all this that he throws it up and goes off to take it out on Edward II.

1415 House of Tudor established, which means exposing beams, restoring inglenooks, enforcing stud walls with RSJs, installing damp courses without structural damage to Listed Buildings, re-thatching, removing all rubbish from site and making good, and so on. A time of great DIY unrest, since materials are short. It is not until Henry VIII demolishes monasteries that enough mullioned windows can be found to satisfy unprecedented demand.

1558 Elizabethan England and flowering of literary renaissance: Bacon's *Cedarwoode Roome Extensciouns Withoute Tears*, Marlowe's *Plummynge on a Groate*, Greene's *Tern Thatte Old Patio into an Ornamental Ponde* and, of course, Shakespeare's extraordinary *Lagge Those Cysternes the Easy Waye Todaye*. Walter Raleigh returns, and roll-your-own is born. The *Golden Hind* circumnavigates the globe, but still cannot find spares.

1605 Guy Fawkes finds prime site in Central London suitable for demolition and redevelopment as executive homes. Planning permission denied. Fawkes attempts to

do it himself anyway. Fawkes topped.

1660 Restoration. Millions of DIY Britons begin stripping pine, removing old veneers, re-upholstering sofas, restoring sideboard doors, replacing table legs, re-glazing breakfront bookcases, etc. Up to nine million pieces of fine furniture irreparably damaged.

1665 Isaac Newton discovers universal principle that anything carried to top of a ladder will immediately fall to the ground.

1748 Twelve-year-old James Watt, while playing with family kettle, completely misses point; which is that not only does no kettle lid fit properly, but that no domestic appliance ever works for more than two days, after which it becomes a device to enable DIY enthusiasts to lose limbs, faculties, and money.

1805 Botch of Trafalgar. One of history's great tinkerers, Nelson, was always trying to make improvements to his ships, losing an eye and an arm in the process. At Trafalgar, insists on going below to sand and polish damaged decks, and is killed when Hardy rolls out of his

Horatio Nelson Patent Gents' Hammock and falls on him. Hardy's last words are: 'Here's another fine mess you've got us into.'

1821 Faraday invents re-wiring. Thousands die.

1840 Postage introduced. DIY enthusiasts now able to send off for millions of mail-order cut-price hammers, saws, pincers, chisels, ladders, drills, spanners, knives, scaffolding, etc. Thousands die.

1850 Prince Albert decides to build greenhouse. Orders extra glass to allow for breakages, wrong measurements, etc.

1851 Too big for Buckingham Palace garden, Crystal Palace erected by Albert in Hyde Park, at enormous cost. Queen Victoria not amused.

1854 Crystal Palace moved by Albert to Sydenham Hill, at even greater cost. Queen Victoria really cheesed off.

1936 Crystal Palace burns down. Queen Victoria turns in grave.

1993 Columnist attempting to replace typewriter ribbon himself is forced to jack in unfinished *History of Jobbing Britain*.

How Beautifully They Stand!

It being the first weekend of spring, that moment when stately home owners throw their premises open to the public, I am delighted to inaugurate an occasional series designed to bring to your attention a few of England's lesser known glories. Today:

BONJOUR CASTLE, Kent.

In 1802, at a bezique-and-cheese party at Emma Hamilton's, Lord Thumlow, Kent's richest landowner, met Horatio Nelson for the first time. The encounter unsettled Thumlow deeply: he was at an utter loss to understand how a dwarf with one arm and one eye could possibly hope to defeat the French.

As the year wore on, he became increasingly glum, convinced that the French would invade and overrun England in a matter of months, and that any resistance to them would be suicidal.

In consequence, instead of bending himself to his official duty of fortifying England's south-east defences, Lord Thumlow built, on the cliffs near Ramsgate, Bonjour Castle, so named because his topiarists had cut the front hedge to form the words in privet letters large enough to be read from Calais with nothing stronger than a pocket telescope.

The castle was designed to conform to standards which Thumlow firmly believed would endear him to the French: there was an ornamental garlic grove, a huge froggery attached to the kitchen garden, a Urinal Keep with accommodation for 800 men, a Suppository West wing equipped with 2,000 bidets, and a nightly torchlit floorshow on the cliffs in which Thumlow's chambermaids danced the can-can clad only in onions, in the hope of storing up goodwill with any invasion fleet which might be heaving-to offshore.

On 22 October 1805, the day after Trafalgar, Lord Thumlow was set upon by patriotic neighbours, put in his new wine-press, and squeezed flat. Bonjour Castle was razed, but the ruins are well worth a visit, especially by escargophiles: there are varieties here so hilariously inbred as to render even the most sober enthusiast helpless.

Nature Notes: April

Blackbirds are hopping about all over. Black birds, anyway. Call it a crow and you won't go far wrong. Soon, the hedgerows will be ablaze with that yellow thing, about the size of a daisy, only different petals and no smell to speak of, you would know it if you saw it. At night, now that the weather is warming up a bit, there's a hell of a racket from something, could be an owl, but less of a hoot, if you know what I mean, more like a squeak than a hoot, might be a mouse of some kind, but up a tree. Forsythia is at its proudest just now, whatever it is. If you are very lucky and quiet, you may catch sight of a horse.

The rivers, winding their immemorial way between banks etcetera, are a-teem with fish. Prominent among these are the big fish, often twice the size of medium fish, and, compared with tiny fish, enormous. If you are patient, you will see them leaping up out of the water at eventide, doubtless surfacing for a look round when they think it is safe. You will not see flat fish, however, because these stay on the bottom on account of not needing to come up for a look round due to having eyes in the back of their head, hence the famous expression.

Quite Unspeakable

Leafing through a Plaid Cymru pamphlet, I was horrified to come across the following paragraph:

Cwll pwm llygbrm ap ngwll Norman Lamont fllyg hwym tillwy Miss Llandudno magwe llwyn hwyt cwm offishwll Jaguar. Ygr dwll fwyn, 36–23–38, llap clewys y plisman, tewyn og myfwy, cwm dywith: 'Well he would, wouldn't he?' Ap tifl biggryl nymmis, ig newy erm difwynn! Cwyllith pwym, eh?

I trust I speak for all of us when I say that such tactics represent an appalling new low in British electioneering. Someone must pay.

When in Rome

Few will have been surprised at Wednesday's announcement that worshippers wishing to see the Pope during his forthcoming Italian tour will have to pay for their seats.

For ours is an era not only of global recession, but also of maximal marketing, and Rome can put two and two together as well as anyone else wishing to make five. Thus it comes about that I have before me *The Bumper Catalogue of Papal Bargains*, just published, in which so abundant is God's bounty that I hardly know where to begin.

Perhaps with the **Fully Extendable Papal Loft Ladder**, available for only £18.95 at all good branches of Rumbelpope's. Originally developed for looking a bit more closely at the Sistine Chapel ceiling, this handsome aluminium item will stand against any wall. When not in use, it can be folded up and used either as handy kitchen steps or simply as something to look at and wonder what it's like when it's unfolded.

Then again, what about a **Genuine Ex-Pope's Trenchcoat**? Due to an ordering oversight by the Vatican, 40,000 of these husky simulated-gabardine bargains, identical to the one worn by serving Popes, are now available to everyone *at less than cost*! They come with unique football-style buttons, he-man belt with integral buckle and holes, and two (2) pockets usually found only on ex-Popes' trenchcoats at twice the price.

You may of course prefer to splash out on **Papal Radiator Shelving**. When His Holiness wishes to avoid nasty brown stains on the Vatican walls while simultaneously having something to stand things on, eg money-box, alarm clock, executive papal toy, he does not go bothering Almighty God, he gets on the blower to Just Divine Chipboard Ltd, and within days he is looking at an elegant addition to his home in fashionable oakette, securely fastened with brass-type brackets which require only the most rudimentary understanding of the hammer to fix. Now he is in a position to pass these on to the general public at only £9 per metre! All items guaranteed to be nearly heat-resistant.

Just an Old Queen, Really

Dr Lillian Schwartz's suggestion that Queen Elizabeth the First might have been William Shakespeare is, of course, utterly ludicrous. While the evidence of the good professor's New Jersey computer (which analysed contemporary portraits of both to arrive at its conclusion) is not in dispute, her interpretation of it has unfortunately grasped the wrong end of the stick with both hands.

I myself have a computer, costing nearly £400, which has enabled me to prove beyond any shadow of a doubt that it was not Queen Elizabeth who put on a false beard to write *Hamlet*, it was William Shakespeare who shaved off a real one to assume the throne of England. That is why he was known as The Virgin Queen in the first place. The first place, incidentally, was the back bedroom of Ye Ratte & Cockie, Southwark, where Sir Walter Raleigh's hair went white overnight.

As a loyal subject, he of course kept his mouth shut, but he was never the same.

A Holidaymaker Writes

Dear Mr Coren,

I hope you will not mind me writing to you, but I saw your face grinning up at me off of my dinner, and you look a sympathetic sort of a person despite having a chip in one eye, also suddenly seeing a bit of *Sunday Express* out here made me think of dear old England etcetera, and I do not know where else to turn, I am at my wit's wossname.

I am on a Greek island, not sure which, I think it ends in *-os*, it has Red Barrel and Big Macs and a Berni Inn, so you can probably identify it on a map. The thing is, I paid £567 in Macclesfield for a Singles Spring Break to meet the man of my dreams as per brochure, but when I got here to see who they had teamed me up with, he was not finished. On the brochure the men of your dreams was all bronzed and muscular with little bums and curly hair, but mine is called Cyril and he is white all over except for his little thin face which is bright red and skinned, he looks like a boiled prawn, and he is virtually bald with no muscles at all, all his bulk is in this big oval backside he's got, which he keeps in a pair of baggy black woollen trunks with the label showing. He has also got a baseball hat with MASONS DO IT ON THE LEVEL round the peak. What I want to know is, have I got a claim against Funsingles (Macclesfield) Ltd? I have complained to the courier on Thingos, and he has promised that a lot of people arrive to find the man of their dreams half-built but not to worry, Cyril will be finished very soon, he will go brown and get his muscles up etc as per brochure, but personally I have my doubts, I have seen better-built stick insects. If I kick up enough of a stink, would they move me to a more developed specimen? Please advise soonest, I am sick of sleeping in the bath, it has got his rubber duck in it, and it quacks when I turn over.

Yours
(name & address supplied)

Royal Appointment with Her Majesty

Following the latest Buckingham Palace security breach, a police spokesman declared that he shuddered to think of what might happen if, some night, the Queen were to come across a burglar in the corridor. Well, I don't shudder at all. I can think of little that Her Majesty is more experienced in handling ...
Good evening.

Good evening, ma'am.
And what do you do?

I do premises, ma'am. I am what the industry calls a Second Storey Man.
How very interesting! What exactly does your work entail?

It entails nipping in, doing the second storey, and nipping out. It is highly skilled work, ma'am. And may I apologize that I do not have a child with me for the purpose of giving your gracious Majesty a bunch of violets? A child would be something of a handicap in my work, it could drop off the guttering and make no end of a bang when it hit the concrete, you could be looking at the wrong end of

three years.
One quite understands.

Also, I am unable to issue you with special clothing. I know you like to wear pit helmets etcetera when visiting workplaces, but I only have the one balaclava with me, due to turning left at Forest Gate.
One begs your pardon?

I should have been doing the New Cross Ladbroke's, only

I turned left instead of right. I did not intend doing your drum at all. If I'd known, I'd have brought a spare balaclava for your own good self. But you can have a go holding my bag.
How very kind! It appears to have SWAG written on it.

It belonged to a cartoonist, ma'am. They often do a bit of moonlighting. Basically you are holding it very well,

though personally I would carry it so's the word SWAG was concealed by my body, pardon the familiarity, so's not to draw wossname to myself.
How clever! And what is this thing with GAS BOARD written on it?

It is a jemmy, ma'am. If stopped, I explain that I am reading meters. It usually convinces the average copper.
Fascinating! Well, one mustn't keep you from your work any longer, it's been most interesting talking to you, but you must be frightfully busy.

That is most considerate, ma'am, I ought to be moving along due to where there is a bloke holding the bottom of a ladder up New Cross who will be sick and tired of explaining to the Old Bill that he is waiting to elope with a bookmaker. May I say it has been a privilege describing my work to your good self? I trust it was of some interest, not too technical?
Not at all. One has been fascinated! A footman will show you to the window.

Something for the Weak End

I am delighted to hear that the Mother's Union has now decided to open its own bordellos. And, having talked to a spokesmother, I am further convinced that all sane people will join me in applauding the scheme unreservedly.

According to her, the MU takes the caring view that more and more British husbands are finding their marital needs inadequately served. This dire situation has sprung from feminism's twin thrusts, economic independence and sexual entitlement: today's husband not only comes home to unkempt premises and a scribbled instruction on the microwave, he is also required, when his wife does eventually return from work, to hurl himself upon her in a hopeless bid to satisfy the demands which the media have persuaded her are her right. No wonder, then, that husbands yearn for other women!

As he enters the typical MU bordello, with its spotless worktops, shining floors, gleaming furniture, and immaculate laundry, the client will find a hot dinner waiting on the table. A dry martini stands beside his plate, a bottle chills in its cooler, and his evening newspaper is warm to the touch from its recent ironing. His cigar lies pierced.

The girl who has done all this will then enter, smelling deliciously of Flash and Windolene, and begin knitting him a nice beige cardigan. Depending on his needs, she will then ask him to talk intimately about the strange knocking in his crankshaft, QPR's decision to play a conventional sweeper, or why his new putter was money down the drain. If he likes dressing up, they can put on overalls and paint the ceiling together.

Should his demands be more out of the ordinary, an extra fiver will bring him a little light sadistic nagging, possibly about not putting a shelf up over the sink, and, for a further tenner, she will initiate a shouting match about her dress allowance which will enable him to cower as much or as little as he needs. If, mind, he is after major humiliation, twenty pounds will buy the entrance of her mother, who will arrive with a suitcase and glare at him for an hour or two.

The session ends with the girl complaining of a headache, allowing the satisfied customer to slip away into the night, his marriage saved.

More Travel Tips: The Ellice Islands

These were formerly the Gilbert & Ellice Islands, until the Act of Severance of October 1975. In the Ellice Islands, the natives speak Ellice, though you can get by on a smattering of Gilbert (*HMS Pinafore* always goes down well with waiters and cabbies).

The country is made up of nine small islands: Nanumea, Nanamunga, Niutao, Nui, Vaitupu, Nukufetau, Nukulaelae, Nurakita, and Funafuti.

Many readers have written to ask me for the quickest means of travel to Nurakita; I suggest you get yourself to Funafuti and then see if anyone's going that way.

The islands are justly famous for their eating. The inhabitants will eat anything. You would therefore be well-advised not to leave your books or Ambre Solaire lying around.

A Villain Writes

Dear Sir,

I note that the new Lord Chief Wossname is in favour of judges ditching their wigs, and I crave the indulgence of your columns to say I hope my esteemed colleagues under the Bench have not got no funny ideas about following suit.

The stocking mask is the badge of our profession. It has been handed down to us since time immoral, and while we have seen the sad demise of the striped jersey and the bag marked SWAG due to cartoonists and other ratbags bringing our robes of office into disrepute, The Nylon, as we call it, has so far remained inviolate. It is a mark of respect: people seeing us coming into a sub-post office or building society know what is expected of them, it is just like calling out 'All Rise!', except of course it is 'All Lie Down!' Take it away, and where are we?

And don't try telling me it is an out-of-date relic of the eighteenth century, eg Dick Turpin with that black velvet number over his eyes, what is wrong with tradition, that is what this country is all about, that is what tourists come here for, if I had to mug a Jap or similar without my nylon on, I wouldn't know where to look, he would not be getting his money's worth, never mind having nothing to tell his grandchildren.

Yours etc

Orient Express

A Chinese sports official has telephoned me from China to say that drug tests carried out on a Yunan 12-year-old girl, who yesterday simultaneously broke world weight-lifting and sprint records by running the 100-metres in 8.4 seconds while carrying a half-ton barbell, have proved negative. I asked him if I might convey this to the AAA and ring him back, but he told me that, sadly, he would not be in his office because he was about to fly to Beijing on the two o'clock pig.

Today's Anniversaries

Cadbury's Fruit and Whelk flopped, 1958. Pope Pius XII taught to juggle by post, 1946. Custer's Third Stand, 1866. Bleriot's luggage lost, 1909. Pedro the Shipping Billionaire bought first boat, 1938. Florence Nightingale drunk in charge of milk-float, 1881. Freddie Mills found half-crown down back of sofa, 1951. William Wordsworth invented doughnut, 1792. Henry V grew another inch, 1417. Bourne made improper suggestion to Hollingsworth, 1931. Sir Alexander Fleming discovered blackhead, 1949. Women's Institute persuaded Hore-Belisha to rename beacon, 1934.

Our Lawyer Advises

First of a new series

Dear Our Lawyer,

It has been suggested that I ought to make a will. Can you tell me the sort of things I ought to watch out for?

Yes. For a start, watch out for anyone suggesting that you ought to make a will. Next thing you know, it'll be ground glass in the Frosties, and cars backing out of the garage sharpish while you are bent down examining a dahlia.

So ignore all suggestions from family, friends, and so forth, and consult a lawyer immediately. Lawyers are trained to be sympathetic and sensitive in all matters concerning clog-popping, and may even be able to put you in touch with a brother in the trade who could give big discounts on tasteful copperene urns etcetera.

As to legacies, you will be aware that a wife is entitled to half her husband's estate, so you would be well-advised to cut her loose at an early stage if you feel she will be down in Marbella on your hard-won capital before the sexton's wiped the mud off his shovel. Many lawyers will give you an attractive divorce 'n' testament package, in which they will get wife's counsel to accept a 25 per cent divorce settlement in return for you and the two lawyers splitting the other 25 per cent up three ways. Leaving money to children can be a big mistake, causing division within the family; there are better ways of causing division within the family without parting with what the law describes as large ones.

Children may also be spoilt by sudden wealth; it is better to leave just a token memento. A tin of beans, say, would not go to anyone's head. As for cats' homes, memorial benches, scholarships for layabouts, etc, you and I are men of the world and do not spend 40 years grafting away so that some wall-eyed ginger tom can dip its face in caviar.

You will, I think, have caught my drift by now: leaving one's estate to one's lawyer represents, surely, the seal on that bond which unites man and client. Your life's earnings will be spent shrewdly, your bereaved ones will be spared the acrimony and grief of shrieking and haggling, and you will, beyond question, get the will itself drawn up dirt cheap.

On a Wing and a Prayer

Am I alone in being horrified by the news from Telford? Telford is taking upward mobility literally. The Shropshire new town is to build a 130-acre housing estate of 64 executive dwellings, each with a private aeroplane hangar so that Telford's executives may commute by wing.

Could any social development be more ominous? Can you imagine how it will be on a Sunday morning in Telford, with 64 poseurs Simonizing their Cessnas before hedge-hopping to the airstrip beside the Rat & Cockle for a lunchtime bevvy and prawn? Can you imagine how it will be inside the pub itself, when these honking dingbats strive to out-do one another with tales of performance and prang and optional extra, with anecdotes of record times to Milton Keynes and Canary Wharf?

Can you imagine how it will be when they are hedge-hopping back after six big gins, cackling that being legless never affected Douglas Bader?

Nor will it stop there: the pecking order of such folk demands that they progress from piston Piper to Learjet, and on, for all I know, to Stealth and Concorde. How long before there are two-plane families, a Mirage in the garage and a helicopter on the roof? And suppose there are only 63 such dwellings? What of the hapless 64th resident, with merely a Porsche to show for all his executive graft, his empty hangar testament to his laughable failure? I give his marriage six months.

As for hotting, the mouth dries and the goose-flesh rises. Mark my words, any day now we shall open our newspapers to find that a mob of Telford adolescents has just carried out a 64-bomber raid on Hamburg.

A Masterspy Writes

Dear Sir,

I can hardly believe it, me writing a letter in visible ink. I feel absolutely gutted, my entire career is up the Swanee, I might as well have gone into my old man's ironmongery, I spent five years learning how to tap 'The grey geese are flying tonight' on a drainpipe so's a bloke on the roof would know it was time to go off and stick a poisoned umbrella into an Albanian, and what has it all come to? It has come to Sir Colin McColl saying, 'Hallo everybody, I am head of MI6, I am top banana in the Unsecret Service, would anyone like to have a butcher's inside my hollow tree to see if there's any messages, har-har!'

Next thing you know, I shall be listed in Yellow Pages under *Spies, Agents and Moles*, I shall have to carry MI6 business cards saying Morris 009 Clitterhouse, 24-Hour Undercover Worker to the Carriage Trade, No Job Too Large or Small, Reasonable Rates, Let Us Quote You, I shall probably have a little van with 'MI6' on the side, instead of an Aston Martin with a Bofors gun in the foglight.

I shall have to have the bungalow completely re-done, you know what it's like when you have to take up floorboards to get short-wave radios out, the Axminster never goes back proper, it goes all wrinkly round the skirtings, not to mention our entire decor theme being based on having binoculars on tripods in every room, plus chandeliers on account of you cannot put a bug in a wall-light, everybody can see it, the wife has always wanted wall-lights and I've got no case now, it'll cost a bomb.

Yours etc
(name & address supplied)

Cheep at Any Price

Like me, you will have seen that the Little Gull and the Mediterranean Gull have been added to the list drawn up under the Protection of Birds Act, but, unlike me, you may not have the faintest idea of what these birds are. Read, therefore, and learn.

Little Gull

As its name implies, this witless bird is a sucker for anything, but is mainly to be found in supermarkets, where it is invariably gulled into going for special offers on unlabelled tinned goods.

Unlike the Big Gull, which believes anything it hears about Prince Edward, the Channel Tunnel, or British Telecom, the Little Gull is conned only by small operations, eg it will listen to double-glazing salesmen for hours, and often flies home with items it has picked out of open suitcases in Oxford Street.

It is despised by other birds, who are always offloading junk on it and telling it porkies. The Little Gull thus believes the recession is coming to an end, and lays its eggs under gooseberry bushes.

Mediterranean Gull

Bigger than the Little Gull, but no brighter, it migrates to the Mediterranean, though frequently fails to arrive, since it asks directions from any bird it passes. Mediterranean Gulls can, as a result, be found anywhere, at any time of year; in 1984, 300 of them spent Christmas in Preston, and a permanent colony now inhabits Rockall in the firm belief that it is Majorca.

Occasionally, however, some do arrive in the Mediterranean, only to discover that they have once again been fooled and that their winter habitat is still half-built, miles from the sea, and that they have to sleep 12 to a nest.

When they examine the small print in their holiday insurance, they invariably find they are indemnified only against cycling accidents.

Our Lawyer Advises: Number 2

Dear Our Lawyer,

Last year, I bought a house in totally unspoilt countryside. I now learn that a new motorway is to go across the garden of the house next door. What on earth am I to do?

I do sympathize. This is rotten luck. Had you bought the house next door instead, you'd be laughing yourself sick now.

Still, it may not be too late; the people next door may be clueless nerds so busy worrying about their loss of amenity that they have not twigged the nature of the goldmine they're sitting on. Your best bet is to flog your house to some unsuspecting hick sharpish, and buy the one next door.

However, it'd be wise to take precautions, just in case a suspecting hick comes along; searches would reveal the projected motorway, so find a lawyer who knows someone in the local planning department. I have found that many of these good folk are prepared to drop things behind filing cabinets in return for used notes, and the motorway could thus remain undetected until well after completion takes place on your property.

Once you have bought the house next door for nothing, you can begin to go to work. With the rise in environmental concern, the Planning Bar has increased a hundredfold, and because its cases are very juicy indeed, barristers like to spin hearings out as long as possible, allowing you to make umpteen improvements to your property – ballroom, pool, tennis court, dog-track etc – thereby giving your lawyer something to get his teeth into when the hearing finally gets to assessing your compensation.

By about 1998, you could be looking at a seven-figure sum, given the right QC.

In the Frame

I have the utmost sympathy for Mr Lester Winward, the Cheshire businessman who bought a painting for £360 in the firm conviction that it was a Raphael worth £10 million but is finding great difficulty in persuading art experts that it is anything but a copy. I have that sympathy not just because £360 doesn't grow on trees, but because of my own experience with the conflicting opinions of the art establishment over my Breughel.

Some years ago, rummaging at a country-house sale, I found a tea tray with a painting on it by Pieter Breughel the Elder. Not only did I recognize the style immediately, the attribution was endorsed, on the back, by a leading Birmingham manufacturer. Astonishingly, I was able to snap it up for a mere 80p, and immediately ran round to Sotheby's to see how many millions I could expect. Their experts were, however, dubious: after examining it for some hours, the majority decision was that the paintings of Breughel the Elder did not normally have handles.

Could it, I suggested, be by Breughel the Younger?

Possibly, they said, but their Breughel the Younger expert had been called out to examine a dishcloth; would I care to leave the painting? Naturally, I demurred, I know these people, they would have had the handles off it in a flash and put it on the next boat to New York, marked *Tractor Spares*. Instead, I took it to Christie's where the view of three experts was that it might be by Breughel the Middle One, who was believed to have used tea stains a lot in his compositions, but the others were doubtful that Breughel the Middle One had ever been to Birmingham, could I perhaps be thinking of his close relative, Breughel the Middle One's Uncle?

I fared no better at either the V & A, who refused to commit themselves to anything but the possibility of its having been nicked from a Flemish tea room by Breughel the Bent, or the Whitechapel Art Gallery, who opened the door only because the man who answered the phone had told them I was coming round with a bagel.

At the time of going to press, I am using it as a tea tray. It seems the simplest course, and one I commend to Mr Winward. Stick a couple of handles on it, and, unlike the experts, you won't go far wrong.

A Dangle-Dolly Writes

Dear Sir,

I approach you, as an influential national commentator and deeply caring person, on behalf of everyone in the dangling industry, in the hope that you will be able to do something to avert the terrible threat dangling over us all. Please forgive the pun, it does not mean I am not dead serious, it is just that I have been put on this earth to amuse mankind, and sometimes I cannot help myself. It is what being a professional is all about.

I am a plastic gonk, and my job is to hang from a rear-view mirror and bob up and down so that my eyes light up when my Ford Sierra drives over a sleeping policeman, kerb, hedgehog, or similar. Not only is it regular work. I also enjoy bringing happiness to people; you would not credit the pleasure I get when my car rings to hysterical laughter as I bang against the blue fur dice dangling beside me, whom, furthermore, I have come to regard not only as professional colleagues, but as close friends. I also get along very well with the titchy luminous St Christopher who stands on the dashboard under us and plays *Ave Maria* when the driver pokes him, although I do not see much of the little alsatian nodding on the back shelf due to where the view of him is generally obstructed by drunks on the rear seat. Nor, unfortunately, have I succeeded in forming a close relationship with Garfield the Cat on account of he is stuck on the side window so that he looks out, not in.

There is, I have been told, another Garfield the Cat on the outside of the car, who appears to have stuck his head through one of the doors, but there is no head inside as far as I can tell, although it may be concealed by the QPR scarf wound into the side window and hanging down next to the drunks, but not so it interferes with the sticker explaining that Essex men do it in their sleep.

You will of course, having heard what we are all in is a Ford Sierra, realize why I am writing to you, because you have read this week that the Sierra has been discontinued. This will mean, quite literally, the end of the road for millions of us in the dangling profession, due to where 97.3 per cent of us work in Sierras.

I beg you to publish this letter and bring our plight to public attention. We are all dangling here, not knowing which way to turn.

Yours etc

Chinese Whispers

Since many of you will have been puzzled not only by the offer of Hong Kong millionaire Li Ka-Shing to buy Canary Wharf when nobody else wanted it, but also by HM Government's eager encouragement of his bid, let me quickly put you out of your bewilderment.

Study the aerial snapshots of the site, and you will immediately see that it bears a remarkable resemblance to Li Ka-Shing's home patch, ie it is a water-girt collection of towering eyesores capable of cramming in thousands of occupants per square foot of territory and, should the necessity arise, sticking umpteen more of them on houseboats.

That necessity, I can now reveal, will arise in 1997, when Hong Kong itself passes into the hegemony of China. It has long been a source of deep humanitarian concern to our caring Government that so many expensive fixtures and fittings will be left in the lurch, but this can now be solved by moving the entire colony to Docklands, leaving nothing behind for the Communists but the odd light-bulb and toilet-roll holder.

As for Li Ka-Shing, not only will he get the whole shebang for a knockdown drag-out price, he will undoubtedly cop a major honour for outstanding services to the Commonwealth. There is even talk of the courtesy title King Kong, though suggestions that he will climax the inauguration ceremony by scaling Canary Wharf Tower are somewhat premature.

Sum Mistake Surely?

Like me, you were no doubt dumbfounded by Monday's Gallup Poll which revealed that 94 per cent of the population believed our politicians to be shifty, untruthful and untrustworthy.

It is a truly astonishing figure. Its implications are incalculable. It frightens the life out of me.

It means that six per cent of the population is barking mad.

Did You Know?

I was delighted to hear from the States that Ripley's Believe It Or Not books were to be updated and revived, particularly because the publishers are soliciting contributions from people who may have come across peculiar facts in the 30 years since the last Ripley appeared, and even more particularly because I myself have long been a collector. Here is just a handful of interesting facts I have come across:

Haddock have a very sophisticated form of radar, but have never worked out how to use it. The smallest diamond ever discovered was the Bloemfontein Speck. Orville Wright had the same dressing-gown for eight years. Mount Everest is almost twice as heavy as Cardiff. The penguin is so called because of its temperament. There is no way of saying 'Deep fine leg' in Flemish. The birthplace of Federico the Weird used to be next door to a cats' home. The surface area of the modern telephone is 131.64 square inches. Out of 18 northern towns, only Rochdale has that name. The Indian Ocean is entirely without corners. The human brain has fewer than six moving parts.

Holiday Tips: New Seasonal Series

No 1: Remember to Tell the VATman You're Away!

Every quarter, thousands of sole proprietors or other duly authorized signatories return home from holiday to find their premises ransacked. It's a sickening feeling when it happens to *your* business – your output files ripped open, your schedules of inputs vandalized, previous months' under-declarations strewn about all over the place, and, perhaps worst of all, both sets of ledgers missing. You may even find that the intruders, thwarted in their bid to come across anything worth taking, have gone through your most intimate spread-sheets and scrawled horrible things on them.

According to one weary Customs & Excise inspector: 'The public never learns. They just go off without so much as a mention to us as to whether they may be importing bonded steam hoists, prosthetic gerbil limbs, partially-coated floor coverings (excluding linoleum), mock-vintage camel saddles, tinned peach halves (stoned), or zero-rated gingerbread men – you name it. They forget that it is the duty of our personnel to make periodic what we term swoops, and if we have reason to suspect that the registree is off out of it, we must naturally effect an immediate forced audit.'

So do remember – unless, before you go away, you make the proper return to Southend-on-Sea SS99 1AA, the heartache of clearing up, not to mention what could be months of readjustments, appeals and banging your head against a brick wall *COULD HAPPEN TO YOU!* And don't forget to ask a neighbour to keep an eye open for those tell-tale buff envelopes which give up to 48 hours' notice of inspection, otherwise, when the worst happens, they may simply assume you've got burglars and not wish to get involved.

Next week: Packing a tortoise.

A Corgi Writes

Dear Sir,

One has had it up to here, one doesn't mind saying. Even as one writes, one knows the gutter Press is already cobbling snide headlines such as YES, BUT HAS ONE HAD IT UP TO HERE RECENTLY? and so on and so forth, one would think they had something better to write about, what about dogs copping it up Sarajevo, what about dogs in the rainforests, there is hardly a decent tree left, what about starving dogs all over Africa, one never sees that reported, does one, oh no, not while there's THOSE GLITTERING CORGIS — IS THERE A RIFT? or HEIR OF THE DOG BARKING MAD, CONFIRMS EXPERT etc, and does one have the right to reply, does one hell, one is only going public now thanks to dictating this through the Buck House railings to an authoritative Airedale close to the Throne, a personal friend, the sort of dog you can rely on to take this to a decent newspaper and not run off to the tabloids with a lot of iffy Polaroids in return for two hundredweight of Kennomeat.

The truth is yes, one does get depressed about not being allowed to make new relationships, it is no joke spending one's entire life among dogs with titchy legs, one has often fancied a nice tall Collie, or maybe something foreign and mysterious like a Borzoi, or a bit of rough, eg a Rottie, but that is not the deal one was brought up to expect, one just has to make the best of it, it is all a matter of breeding, not that there is much of that, that is what makes one sick about such headlines as WOT, NO NEW PUPPIES, SEE CENTRE SPREAD FOR EXCLUSIVE PICTURES OF SEPARATE KENNELS! or ROYAL CORGI GAY SHOCK! it does not seem to have occurred to them that her indoors is very particular about all that, as a matter of fact my bitch and I get on very well, we go our own way, true, my hobby is digging up old bones, hers is scratching, but we always spend Christmas together, ask anyone.

One's etc

How Shakily They Stand

Following Tuesday's news that the National Trust is to stop advertising some of its most popular properties because it fears they are being harmed by the feet of too many visitors (the floor of Kipling's house, Bateman's, recently collapsed), I thought it time to bring you the long-promised Part Two of my series on less popular stately homes, in the hope that traffic may thus be diverted from the endangered ones. This week, therefore:

SHELDON ABBEY,
Hendon

Sheldon Abbey, built on the site of an original Erzanmine Developments Executive Mansionette, *circa* 1967, is that remarkable rarity in English sacred architecture, an abbey built by a blouse manufacturer.

In 1972, Harry Sheldon and his wife, Queenie, having taken a wrong turning on the A303 when bound for Bournemouth, found themselves at Glastonbury. They were immediately captivated by the abbey ruins. Queenie particularly liked the way the living room had a grass floor, it meant you didn't have to spend a fortune on house plants, your only problem was worms getting stuck in the Hoover, while Harry was delighted with the way you could drive the Jag straight into the master bedroom, it meant you could come home drunk from charity functions without having to fiddle about looking for your keys. They returned to Hendon, and without more ado began to convert their house accordingly.

Problems did not arise until they attempted to convert Queenie's father to match: retired now from the launderette industry and living upstairs in what the Sheldons intended to turn into the organ loft, he maintained that he was too old to become a monk, not only would he not be able to carry on wearing his homburg indoors, shaving a hole in his head could bring on a terminal chill.

Thus faced with an insoluble dilemma (the old man owned 51 per cent of Harry's business), the Sheldons put the abbey on the market in 1973, and moved to a flat overlooking Regent's Park. The abbey remains unsold, for some reason, to this day, but squatters have opened it to the public between 2 pm and 6 pm on Sundays, and it is well worth the 50p just to hear the carillon play *If I Were a Rich Man.*

Not for the Squeamish

I was greatly relieved at Friday's announcement that the BBC had introduced guidelines on violence, and would henceforth preface contentious broadcasts with a health warning. This, I understand, will read: 'The following programme was commissioned by John Birt over someone's dead body. Viewers of a sensitive disposition should switch off and go down to the pub.'

Our Lawyer Advises: Number 3

Dear Our Lawyer,

A few days ago, I opened a bottle of milk purchased at a local supermarket and found a mouse inside it. What should I do about this?

It is interesting that you do not say: 'I opened a bottle of milk and found to *my horror* a mouse inside it.' That is the form we in the legal profession strongly recommend. If it was not to your horror, what exactly *was* it to? If, for example, it was to your delight, then I fear I am ethically bound to advise you that there is little we can do to screw the shop for every penny. Indeed, it could well be in your interest to write a note of thanks to the shop, enclosing a cheque to protect yourself against any claim on the shop's part for its mouse back.

If, though, it was merely to your surprise, then there may well be a bob or two in it, depending of course on the extent of your surprise; far be it from me to put ideas into your head, but if the surprise was such that you fell back against a priceless Ming vase which, as it shattered, caused your prize chihuahua to snuff it, then compensation could be considerable. If, however, you merely exclaimed: 'Stone me, it's a mouse!' I do not see much material advantage in your going to court.

Nor do you say whether or not the mouse was dead. If it left the shop alive and died while in your charge, you could well find yourself facing an action for cruelty, with the result that you might be prohibited for life from keeping another mouse. Were this the case, we in the legal profession would not wish to touch you with what we call a bargepole.

Why not write me another letter, along the lines of: 'I recently opened a bottle of milk purchased at a local supermarket, and to my inexpressible horror and disgust found a dead mouse inside it, since when I have had no sleep, suffered fainting fits, eaten nothing, and lost all sexual interest. Can you in the legal profession take the shop to the cleaners, not just for me, but for decent human beings everywhere?'

A Horse Writes

Dear Sir,

Until recently, I was the only one the Prince of Wales played polo on. Now he appears to have gone off me, and I do not know which way to turn (no pun intended). The thing is, close friends up the stable say there is a book in this, I ought to tell my side, they would all be keen to collaborate, you would not credit some of the stories. But the problem is you cannot hoof a typewriter, all the keys come up together. It has taken me three days just to write this, holding a Biro in my teeth.

What I would like to know is, would you be prepared to type it if we dictated? I know you speak fluent pony, and we could easily be looking at a six-figure advance here, never mind serial rights.

Yours etc

A Prime Minister Writes

Dear Sir,

May I crave the indulgence of your very interesting columns to add my personal regrets at the most untimely death of mild-mannered reporter Clark Kent? I was really quite taken aback when I read that DC Comics Incorporated, of the United States of America, had decided to, as they were pleased to put it, 'kill off Superman'. It was a most disagreeable decision on their part. A lot of people will have been very put out by it. Oh yes.

Mr Kent, I believe I am correct in saying, was considerably unique. I have been a great fan of his ever since I was quite a small boy, when my imagination — like that of many people large and small, young and old, and if you will bear with me for just a moment, tall and short — was agreeably engaged by the idea that someone was prepared to call himself something very silly like Superman and fly about all over the place in long underwear until some turn of events called upon him to go into a telephone kiosk and change into a smart grey suit and nice horn-rimmed spectacles and come out with a completely different name, so that nobody would know who he was and he could get on with his very important job.

Truly, Clark Kent was a

wonderful invention. Until he came along, you may be interested to know, there were really not very many mild-mannered heroes in comic books. In American ones, nearly all the important people were bulletproof and could throw motor cars about and so forth, for example Captain Marvel and Wonderlady and the one with a bat's head, and you could not believe in any of them, they were not at all realistic. It was even worse in English comics, if you will allow me to continue, they had a talking ostrich and a talking cat and an unshaven man who could eat a pie with a whole cow in it, quite incredible. I lived in Brixton, you know, and I never saw anybody like that walking around. I am sure I should have got to hear about a talking ostrich.

But Clark Kent was most

special. He would come out of the telephone box and go off to work with a striped tie on like a real person, and everybody thought he was a very nice man. He had a way of pushing his spectacles up his nose with one finger which was most realistic. When I say he pushed his spectacles up his nose, I do not of course mean up the inside of his nose, that would have been most unacceptable, I mean up the outside, that is to say starting from the end of it and working towards the bridge of it. I hope I have made that quite clear.

He did his job at the newspaper very well. He was not flashy or noisy, his door was always open to reasonable people, he did not flap even when, for example, meteors looked as if they might be about to inflict considerable damage

on the Earth, he did not allow things to get on top of him, he was a model of restraint and a splendid example to people. I well remember going to buy my first pair of brown leather shoes with my own money and insisting that they had eight lace-holes in, just like Clark Kent's. Or, to be quite specific, 16 lace-holes; that is to say, eight each. Four on each side of the tongue. Well, where the tongue would be if you could see it, which of course you cannot do once the laces have been done up.

But now he has gone, and I am quite considerably put out. Nor do I accept DC Comics's explanation that they got rid of him because of market forces. That is a most unsatisfactory excuse, I always think.

Yours etc

Lucky for Some

Intrigued by Monday's report that 83 per cent of us were superstitious, I was annoyed that it didn't specify what we were superstitious about. I have thus decided to remedy this with a brief list.

CATS: the association of cats with luck dates from the period when Egyptians worshipped the cat as a god. A practical people, they realized that having a god who caught mice was a sensible move. Today, many superstitions still surround the cat: it is, for example, unlucky to have a cat which strops its claws on Sheraton sideboards, while many believe that a black cat suddenly running in front of your car is a sign of panel-beating to come.

RABBIT'S FOOT: carrying a rabbit's foot is not particularly lucky, unless you like having a pickpocket vomit on your shoe.

LADDERS: a ladder leaning against a wall can be interpreted as meaning that your silver has been nicked, but more commonly it should be taken as a sign that the plasterer has walked through a door, knocking a painter off a scaffold who has then fallen onto an electrician whose jogged drill has holed a mains pipe, resulting in conditions giving them no option but to leave the ladder where it is and go round to the pub.

HORSESHOES: horseshoes are traditionally associated with extremely bad luck, such as an odds-on favourite getting beaten by a neck.

SEVEN: the number 7 is held to be extremely lucky, though God knows why. Having 7 fingers can be taken to mean you are very unlucky with car doors, having 7 wives indicates that the only lucky thing about you is your lawyers, walking 7 miles is a sign that your fuel gauge requires attention, and having 7 hairs means that stupid people will mistake you for Bobby Charlton. Clever ones will mistake you for Robert Robinson.

THE NEW MOON: it is very unlucky to turn your money over under a new moon. The last sound you hear will be the whistle of short lead pipe. If you have to turn it over at all, choose a full moon, that way you may at least be able to pick out your assailant from an identity parade. Looking at a new moon through glass is also said to be unlucky, though not invariably. If you have a short lead pipe on you, you may be lucky enough to spot some fool standing out there turning his money over.

BEETLES: the belief that treading on a beetle brings bad luck is very common, especially among beetles.

Our Lawyer Advises: Number 4

Dear Our Lawyer,

I am terribly worried about our son. He is still only 17, but has already appeared in court five times on fraud charges. He has misrepresented himself as a Nigerian oilman in order to beguile £50 from an aunt who didn't recognize him under the boot-polish, he took £90 in on-the-spot fines from jaywalking tourists, he persuaded our bank to sponsor him on a 6,000-mile jog to save the grebe but he never went anywhere, he sold a three-year lease on the Cenotaph to a group of Tongan diplomats, and only last month he extracted six wisdom teeth for cash at his road-side dental stall. I have consulted a social worker and a psychiatrist but nobody could help. I am desperate. What legal advice can you offer?

I sympathize utterly. When one has a brilliant son it is hard to pick the career which will maximize his potential. You were mistaken to approach a shrink, the training is very expensive, even though your son sounds the sort of boy able to find a medical school willing to toss him for tuition, and as to social work, the pay is lousy, and never comes in used notes. But you were quite right to approach me. On the evidence, he would make a great lawyer, though which branch only you can decide: if he is merely shifty, article him to a solicitor, but if he is as glib as his achievements suggest, go for the bar. Avoid the corporate path, though: none of his work has netted more than a two-figure sum, and no company would put a lawyer on the board until he had pulled off a six-figure job, preferably in Lichtenstein.

An Author Writes

Dear Sir,

I note with interest that the film rights of both *Diana: Her True Story* and the Duchess of York's *Budgie the Helicopter* books have been sold this week for huge sums, also that one of them has been snapped up by merchandisers of cuddly toys, T-shirts, and so forth, though I cannot remember which, it is probably the former, no one would want a furry helicopter whereas a Princess of Wales dangle-dolly would clearly grace any Ford Fiesta or similar.

My interest in this is that I have been a major author for many years, eg my delightful range of children's books featuring the lovable Winkle the Washing Machine and all the hilarious adventures that happen to him while he is getting out deep-down dirt etcetera, Winkle the Ashtray and all the hilarious people he meets while they are stubbing fags out on him, Winkle the Microwave and all the hilarious songs he sings while irradiating mince, and Hoover the Winkle and all the hilarious problems he has as the result of being a shellfish who believes he can suck muck off the top of pelmets.

I have also written *Tracy: Her True Story*, which is all about a woman with a rotten marriage due to where her husband keeps going on about the state of the house, where's my clean underwear, God this place stinks of fags, stone me not bloody radioactive mince again, these pelmets are filthy, etcetera etcetera, but the thing is none of these books of mine has ever been published due to, not to put too fine a point on it, nobody giving a monkey's, and what I want to know is, is there anything in the constitution which says that, when they are back on the market, Prince Charles or Prince Andrew cannot marry a housewife from Potters Bar?

I have the feeling it would boost my career no end.

Yours etc

Tinker, Tailor, Soldier, Twit

Now that KGB documents have proved that Oxford as well as Cambridge was a hotbed of traitors and spies, it cannot be long before the cover is also blown on Britain's redbrick universities – which of course earned that name for similar activities, even if these were, as one would expect, slightly less distinguished.

Strathclyde, for example, planted a mole in Riga, but his knowledge of Morse went only as far as the letter G and he was thus unable to contact Philby, Maclean, Blunt, or Burgess. He did manage to get through to an agent called Bede, but as his own name was Wilkins, he was unable to tell Bede who he was.

A worse fate befell the two Loughborough Apostles who, having infiltrated M16, were dropped into East Germany. Finding it impossible to get by on their grant, they dug up their parachutes and attempted to sell them, whereupon they were arrested as black marketeers by treble agents from the Northampton Polytechnic, who then found themselves unable, despite their slide rules, to work out whose side anybody was on, and shot them just in case.

Nobody knows quite what happened to the student from Hornsey Art School whose charred skeleton was found welded to an elm outside Omsk, but it is believed that he made the novice's mistake of trying to poke a message into a hollow tree during a thunderstorm.

A House Mite Writes

Dear Sir,

You probably don't remember me — as you will no doubt have read this week, there are three million of us in your mattress alone, and I know you have a bit of a job putting names to faces — but I recently spent the night in your left nostril with a few thousand close friends (it was my wife's birthday) and what with one thing and another the dancing got a bit out of hand, bringing on a fairly major sneeze on your part.

I apologize for waking you up on that occasion, but what I am anxious to know is, have you still got the Kleenex? The thing is, we have been unable to trace the wife's brother, and since it is three days now and it is not like him to wander off without a word, we are afraid he may be in a bin somewhere.

If you wish to get in touch, I expect to be down your ear sometime next Tuesday, and would be grateful for any information.

However, if you cannot help, but think that one of your readers might be able to, perhaps you would be kind enough to publish this in your highly popular and always enjoyable column.

Yours etc

Our Lawyer Advises: Number 5

Dear Our Lawyer,

In June 1984, a tree root from next door's garden grew through the side of our new polystyrene pond, causing subsidence to a gnome. My neighbour refused to compensate me, and my solicitor sought counsel's advice. He recommended I go to court, where the case book took five days, mainly because a number of what my counsel described as fascinating legal points were involved, and I lost. Costs ran to five figures.

Being short of money, I sought time to pay, and took a second job as a nightwatchman, where after three days I was struck on the head by a baseball bat. The company sacked me, and counsel insisted I sue them for unfair dismissal. At the hearing, it transpired I had been asleep when struck on said head; the dismissal was upheld, and costs were given against me. They were also given against me in the case I was advised to bring against my other employer who had dismissed me from my day job on the grounds that I had been off work for two weeks attending a hearing about being unfairly dismissed from my second job.

Now unemployed, I could not find work due to pains in baseball-batted head. My barrister sought compensation from the Criminal Injuries Board, unsuccessfully, for which I had to pay him a huge fee. I was forced to sell my house, but did not get as much as I had hoped because of legal fees involved, and since my wife did not fancy living in one room, she left me and sued for divorce on grounds of cruelty.

My lawyer strongly recommended that I defend the action, which I lost, costs being awarded to my wife, and as I left the court I tripped on a broken paving-stone and dislocated my hip. My barrister instantly initiated a negligence suit against Westminster Council, who not only won, but also successfully counterclaimed on the grounds that my hip had struck a litter-bin as I fell which was damaged beyond repair.

So was my hip; but the Medical Defence Union, defending the doctor I had been advised to sue for malpractice, employed three QCs, and I had no chance, since I was now bankrupt and could afford only to defend the action myself. The case took three weeks, due to all the time I spent limping backwards and forwards across the court as witness and counsel.

What I want to know is, is it possible to sue a barrister?

NO.

DIY Corner:
A New Reader Service

In a recent will, I was left a pair of rubber frog-feet, as well as the 1948 edition of the Shorter Oxford Dictionary. As I am not a swimmer, I was wondering whether they could be converted into normal walking shoes, and if so is it a job for an expert? I am quite good with my hands, and have made a vase out of a hat by lining it with Polyfilla and painting it lilac.

JS Gummer,
Acton

It isn't clear from your letter what exactly it is that you wish to turn into normal walking shoes. If it's the frog-feet, the answer is yes, but be prepared for ill-informed ribaldry. The job itself is simple: the heels may be built up with pieces of old hotwater bottle, and you can draw fairly authentic laces on the uppers with a felt-tipped pen. You would be well advised not to run anywhere, though.

However, if it's the two-volume Shorter Oxford Dictionary to which you are referring, the task is somewhat trickier, as Volume 1 (A-M) is 80 pages shorter than Volume 2 (N-Z), and the conversion, if not professionally carried out, could leave you with a nasty limp. You will, though, be 4 inches taller and may feel this to be adequate compensation; but to do a perfect job, glue a copy of the 80-page Argos catalogue to your Volume 1 shoe, thereby creating a pair of matched clogs that will be a joy to own. Bind them to your feet with sash cord, and do remember to fasten the covers of the books together; there is nothing more embarrassing for a walker than to have his footwear constantly falling open at bizarre definitions.

Adult Entertainment

I confess to being puzzled at the defence plea by Mr Colin Buckland, the insurance broker convicted last week of assaulting kissogram girl Donna Keigher.

He claimed that when she appeared at his 40th birthday party carrying a cane, he thought she was going to whack him with it, and therefore lashed out at her in panic because he had a rash on his bottom to which six of the best would do no good at all.

But were that indeed the case, surely he would not have gone to the party at the Royal Oak hotel without a note from his mother to the manager explaining his condition and excusing him from corporal punishment?

Going on, possibly, to say that he had also had a recent bilious attack, and didn't have to eat his jelly all up, or play musical chairs, because it might very well bring on one of his nosebleeds.

That said, mind, I thought the fine of £500 a bit strong. Had I been the judge, I should have given him 100 lines, made him pick up all the lolly sticks in the court's car-park, cancelled his *Beano* for a month, and sent him straight to bed without any supper.

Opening for Business

Hearing that the recession was forcing private medicine into fierce price-cutting competition, many readers have written to ask what the effect will be. I can do no better than offer this case history from a recent British Medical Journal.

At 11.34 am on 4 May, 1992, a white 48-year-old male crawled up the steps of the Harleywelling Hospital, W1, and collapsed in the foyer.

Mr BJ Hickmore, a consultant surgeon who happened to be in the foyer monitoring Teledata inquiries about his Varicose Family Weekend Offer, immediately ran across and examined the patient for a coupon snipped from any 16-oz jar of Maxwell House Platinum Blend entitling the bearer to £50 off any item of abdominal surgery, provided it was carried out before 30 May by Mr BJ Hickmore.

It was while the surgeon was going through the lining of the patient's bloodstained trilby that he was hurled aside by Dr P Narbley, who had just returned from a TV-am interview concerning his revolutionary technique for giving away a five-gallon can of Havoline with

I'm alright doctor, but this food blender you gave me last visit is playing up wicked

every rectal dilation.

Critical

Dr Narbley slapped the patient awake to inform him that his *opération du jour* was a valuable squint correction at the knockdown price of £250, carrying not only a voucher saving £25 on any prosthetic limb in the Narbley Mail Order Catalogue, but also a scratch 'n' sniff token which, when matched with one from any other piece of minor surgery, would entitle holder to a sun-soaked holiday for two on the fashionable Bosnian Riviera, or a sun-soaked holiday for one in the event of the operation proving unsuccessful, in which case the second holiday could be exchanged at any hospital displaying the Narbley sticker for a new nose or breast, worth £££s.

The exchange of opinion between the two doctors was on the point of becoming critical for the patient — who had during the course of their deliberations been thrown off operating trolleys belonging to four competing stretcher companies — when a clinical team from J Walter Saatchi arrived to announce that the agency had been retained by Dr JF Bannerjee to market a new range of surgical procedures which could be carried out in the comfort of Dr Bannerjee's own van, thereby greatly reducing overheads, especially as the surgical teams were all members of the Bannerjee family and could thus keep the van open cheaply at all hours, particularly if the grocery side was a bit slack after midnight.

Hickmore and Narbley thereupon broke off their examination and went off to discuss the surgical implications with the hospital accountants, leaving the patient propped against the hospital's flower stall, returning to find he had been whisked into theatre by Dr M Hurst, who had spotted him from the bus window.

The operation was a complete success: the kidney fetched £325, a by-pass yielded 14 ft of re-usable intestine @ £4.95 per ft, two pints of blood went for £38, and a cornea achieved a record £200. The patient recovered fully, and was really quite taken with his monocle.

No Holds Bard

Many parents, I know, are horrified at John Patten's insistence that Shakespeare be part of the National Curriculum, because they fear his work will be beyond the capabilities of the modern 14-year-old. They need not worry. I have had a sneak preview of next summer's GCSE paper, and believe it will be within the grasp of at least a few of them.

1. Taking a groat to equal 4p, if Mr and Mrs William Shakespeare went into a McDonald's for two portions of Chicken Mcnuggets, two large fries, and two mango shakes, what would it cost them, to the nearest groat? (*You may use a calculator.*)

2. If Hamlet (not the cigar, the Prince of Denmark) had been picked for their recent European Cup-winning squad, who would you have left out?

3. *The Bill* (ITV) is not about Shakespeare. So what is it about?

4. In one of Shakespeare's top soaps, incredible though it may seem to us, Juliet is 14 when she first goes to bed with Romeo. Taking care not to read the play, try to guess, in your own words, what took her so long.

5. 'He never broke any man's head but his own, and that was against a post when he was drunk' (*Henry V*). Roughly how much would that normally take, in your case? (*You may use a crate of lager.*)

6. *King Lear*, another Shakespeare one, contains no modern swear words. If he was writing it for BBC2 today, which ones do you think he would choose? (*You may use an aerosol.*)

Our Lawyer Advises: Number 6

Dear Our Lawyer,

I should like a divorce, but I cannot prove anything against my husband, I am just sick of his face looking at me from behind things. What do I need to persuade the court that my marriage has broken down irretrievably?

What you need to persuade the court that your marriage has broken down irretrievably is a lawyer.

The changes in the Divorce Laws were introduced expressly to make these unsavoury matters easier for lawyers, who, in the bad old days, often spent years listening to ghastly people whingeing on about their spouses.

Frequently, we ourselves had to go to the bother of appointing private detectives charged with invading cherished privacy, or actually find unscrupulous women prepared to spend the night in tatty hotels with clients solely to enable us to trump up bogus misconduct charges.

Worse, we were sometimes forced to the repugnant lengths of taking incriminating photographs of decent human beings who wanted nothing more than to get their leg over in peace and quiet.

Needless to say, all this filled the legal profession with disgust: there is nothing worse than watching unqualified people — gumshoes, photographers, hotel staff — cleaning up, when the rest of us have spent years studying for expensive degrees. If I had my time over again, I used to think, I'd buy a Polaroid and an old mac, and to hell with sitting around in pinstripes, waiting to divvy up the take . . . Fortunately, the new divorce procedures have changed all that.

To put the legal niceties into a nutshell for the layman, what the latest legislation means is that lawyers get it all, and get it quickly.

We do not have to listen to long, boring stories about how she gets drunk and thumps him with the bedside table, or how he was seen running out of a house up the road with only his socks on, we do not have to spread the jam around to private eyes and iffy escorts and greedy chamberpersons, all we require is a note from you saying you are sick of his face looking at you from behind things and several more notes saying I Promise To Pay The Bearer Fifty Pounds, and we shall do the rest.

An Avocado Writes

Dear Sir,

Many of your readers no doubt believe that the working life of an exotic pear is all beer and skittles.

Oh yes, very nice, they will say, dead cushy, an avocado does not have to stand all the way from Orpington to Charing bloody Cross, day in, day out, it does not have that bastard Warburton in Foods Forward breathing down its neck, it is not required to take a ton of work home in order to keep abreast of developments in systems analysis, it does not have to lie awake all night sweating about whether its career path is likely to be sideswiped by that ferret-faced little schemer they transferred from Halifax, or whether the company's pension fund is going belly up, all it has to do is sit kipping on a nice warm shelf in Sainsbury's, quietly going ripe.

These people do not realize that hardly ten minutes pass without some ratbag picking you up, squeezing your head, and sticking you back again. Is it any wonder we are all dead set against Sunday opening?

Sunday is the only chance an avocado gets to have a bit of a lie-in, nobody poking you, nobody sniffing you, and no chance of ending up took home and stuck on a plate with a couple of dozen dead prawns all over you.

I have nothing personal against Michael Howard, he is no more of a clown than the next Home Secretary, but if any of your readers could see their way clear to pushing the bastard under a bus, they have my personal assurance that few avocados would stand in their way.

Yours etc

Himmler Wrote Something Simmler

I am delighted to be able to tell you that the *Sunday Express* has not only secured the exclusive serial rights to *Joseph: His True Story*, it has managed to persuade me to translate it for the knockdown, drag-out price of only £200,000.

I normally charge far more, being a top political historian (*Adolf of Sunnybrook Farm, Goering-the-Pooh, William Joins the SS*, and many other favourites), but I have a bit of spare time on my hands due to where contracts have not yet been exchanged on my new Christmas CD, *Val Doonican Sings Horst Wessel*, and there could well be a nice little spin-off or two: Dustin would make a wonderful Goebbels, and what about Vera Lynn as Eva Braun? A real show-stopper if Tim and Andrew

could be tempted to get together again.

Terrible

The book, which we shall begin serializing next Sunday, tells for the first time the riveting inside story of Joseph's disastrous marriage, from the heartbreaking moment on his wedding night when Mrs Goebbels went off to play the cello, to that terrible day when he discovered that she had become infatuated with the stunningly handsome world foxtrot contender, Lew Grade.

It was at that moment that Joseph Goebbels, after throwing himself through a cocktail cabinet and running round to Hitler's house to play gin rummy, decided to devote his life to the betterment of mankind, determined not to rest until every poor blond blue-eyed person had a long black leather trenchcoat, big shiny boots, a Luger and a Polish paperweight.

Harrowing

Authenticated by the personal testimony of authoritative sources close to the bunker, with no motive but the revelation of the truth — Mengele, Heydrich, Hess, Eichmann, Ribbentrop, and many more — this harrowing story is essential reading for everyone who cares deeply about newspaper circulation. Don't miss part one, or you'll kick yourself!

(If you are unable to kick yourself, please contact me at this address. We have ways of sending someone round to kick you.)

Our Lawyer Advises: Number 7

Dear Our Lawyer,

I see that the legal profession is strongly opposed to next month's re-imposition of stamp duty. May I congratulate you on the wonderful humane stand the law is taking on behalf of house-buyers everywhere?

Of course you may. There is no law against a person making a prat of himself in a personal communication with his lawyer.

What you should have congratulated us on, of course, was the wonderful humane stand the law is taking on behalf of itself: as you know, there are four things a lawyer can do for you when it comes to house-purchase, (a) Almost Nothing, (b) Virtually Nothing, (c) Next To Nothing, and (d) Nothing. In the first category is deposit-holding, (b) covers searches, (c) is conveyancing itself, and (d) concerns the payment of stamp duty. We have always hated (d), because clients tend to ask what it's for, and we are bound to reply 'Nothing' which often leads clients to ask us about (a), (b), and (c), with their attendant embarrassments.

When the Government suspended stamp duty, clients thankfully stopped asking questions; bringing it back represents a threat not only to all we have and hold, but to all we want to have and hold.

And, yes, lawyers *do* wish to encourage house-buying, not just for (a), (b), and (c), but for everything up to about (t), which covers what happens *after* the house is bought, including things not found in the search — new motorway through garden, old mine shaft under kitchen, planning permission for piggery next door, factory chimney interfering with ancient lights, proposed MoD firing range opposite — all of which may take many years to sort out and bring great benefits, albeit not necessarily to the householder.

That is why lawyers stand united in opposing the iniquitous stamp duty. It is quite appalling the Government should get so much for doing so little.

My Old Man's Adopted

Noting that Virginia Bottomley had not yet responded to observations that, if her Health of the Nation paper produced the desired results, there would be a vast increase in the elderly, and what did the Government intend to do about this, I immediately sought an exclusive interview, and was rewarded with the following:

'I'm so glad you asked that, Alan! Our aim is to encourage the adoption of little old men. Once our plans to reduce pregnancy have borne fruit (rather than anything else), we believe that the childless will be crying out for something to bring up and fuss over.

'Little old men are clean, house-trained, understand words, and do not get you up in the night for a drink, unless they are little old drunks, which we shall do our best to eliminate at an early stage. Nor do little old men constantly grow out of things, although, admittedly, things sometimes grow out of *them*, or cost anything in school fees. Also, they will not give you lip, because they know what a swift clip round the ear can do to someone of 90.

'Furthermore, they do not need teeth, throw their spoons about, stick rusks in the cat's eye, or demand to watch *Play School* while Ascot is on the other channel, and may generally be relied upon to burp without assistance. They will not grow up to want mountain bikes, Nintendo, or crack, and are unlikely to knock about with unsuitable girls or borrow the car, except to lean on for a bit of a cough.'

Since this all seemed straightforward enough, I asked the Minister the one outstanding question, ie what would happen if the little old man didn't like his new parents, and changed his mind? She gave me one of her famously radiant smiles.

'We would send a big old man round to help him change it back again,' she said.

A Bit of a Flutter

Not unexpectedly, baffled entymologists throughout the country have been ringing me up for an explanation of the unprecedented swarms of butterflies which have suddenly begun descending on fields and gardens, enraging farmers, distressing householders, creating havoc and devastation, and offending decency by not only coupling in the open air, but also, as a result, irresponsibly laying millions of unwanted offspring who will doubtless grow up to carry on the anti-social work, having no other example than their parents. Whereupon, having done their worst, the mobs move on, leaving ruin in their wake, to find their next hapless billet. The police are powerless.

The answer, of course, is that these are New Age Butterflies. Encouraged, no doubt, by what they have seen on television (indeed, in all probability, doing it to get on television), they clearly consider themselves to be free spirits, above the law and deferring to nobody. Quite what decent citizens can do about all this remains uncertain, but I fear that bloody confrontation is imminent: only yesterday, I saw a respectably dressed man, possibly a Rotarian, roll up his *Financial Times* and swat a cabbage white in broad daylight.

Anarchy is but a short step away.

New stars, no 7

Hopcroft's Cobblers: many astronomers have attempted to determine what a heel-bar is doing in outer space, but none has succeeded, least of all its discoverer, Sir Desmond Hopcroft, who believes his brown brogues are up there and wants to know when they'll be ready. Since he has been in Broadmoor since 1947, where he will not be allowed shoes even if they turn up because of what he might do with the laces, it is hard to understand why he is so upset, but should he be reading this, it may be some comfort to hear that in my opinion, and I used binoculars, it is not a heel-bar at all. It could be a tobacconist's, but I would not put money on it.

Running for Cover

A Lloyd's name, who shall be nameless (and rather wishes he'd thought of being it a bit earlier), has written saying that in order to make ends meet, he is writing a book on insurance, and can I tell him when it all began?

Yes. While it is impossible to fix an exact date for the birth of insurance, most authorities agree that it was probably discovered by accident, the favoured theory being that our earliest ancestors found, on rubbing two sticks together, that their tree burned down.

Later, one of them was run over by a funny-shaped rock which for some unknown reason suddenly rolled downhill, and the idea really took off. We know this from cave-paintings which show men pursuing mammoths and waving large pens; the men are clearly attempting to interest the mammoths in a policy insuring them against extinction, while the mammoths are running away on the grounds that they would rather spend the money on double glazing.

A Pork Pie Writes

Dear Sir,

I have worked for British Rail for some years now, and I write to express my shock and disgust at the cavalier way in which loyal employees like me are being kept totally in the dark about the upcoming privatization.

A cheese sandwich of my acquaintance tells me he has seen nothing like it since 1983 when, after long and dedicated service in the West Midlands, he and his tomato were summarily transferred to Network South-East without so much as a by-your-leave.

The only information we get is what we can manage to overhear in the buffet. This was how I learned that a Japanese consortium has already snapped up the London–Aberdeen Sleeper, which it intends to run as an itinerant short-time hotel, stopping at every station between the termini to take on dodgy couples prepared to pay £25 for half an hour in the sidings.

Speaking as a senior pork pie, I should not wish to be party to such carryings-on, and I can only hope the buffet car will continue as

Don't look now, but I have a feeling the pork pie has been listening to our entire conversation

per usual to be taken off at Watford due to ants on the line at Doncaster, to spare embarrassment to all.

Likewise the new Nat Rumbelow & Hedges Football Specials, which I understand will cater for away fans who have no interest in the game but just like belting one another.

For the loss-leading fare of only £3, they will be able to travel two miles from Euston where the train will be parked to allow them to get on with it, encouraged by the eight buffet cars full of lager via which the owners will net enormous profits.

But what, I ask, is being done to protect comestibles? Being rock-hard, many of us could well find ourselves being used as deadly weapons and hauled before the beak as accessories, never mind getting bunged through a plate glass window and ending our days halfway up a cutting, covered in flies.

Personally, I would rather take my chances at Fenchurch Square Garden, which I understand is being hired out for New Age Traveller Acid House parties, or even the 8.14 chain of soft-core video outlets now standing at platform 4, but will anyone consult me, will they hell!

Yours etc

A Confused Holidaymaker Writes

Dear Sir,

As a kitchen extractor hood consultant, I meet all sorts, plus a different stratum altogether at my bonsai tree circle (Tuesdays). Furthermore, collecting peculiar headlines, eg MAN HAD TURTLE UNDER CARDIGAN, has taught me, over the years, that life does not hold many surprises for the person who keeps his wits about him.

However, I have been followed to our holiday chalet in Jaywick Sands by a ginger stoker with a medallion and a strange walk whom we parked next to in a lay-by on the A603 to allow our youngest, Cilla, to bring up a whelk. You will gather from this that I am a family man, and nothing like this stoker has ever happened to me before, except a man on the upper deck with a labrador when I was a scout, and I called the conductor and that was the end of it.

The thing is, though, that he has an interest in midget trees, unlike my wife Yvonne, who cannot stand anything Jap. I know this, because he followed me when I went down The Three Jolly Gummers on our first night and he started a conversation, and I did not want to appear prejudiced, after all he might want a kitchen extractor hood one day, you never know in my line. But after I got launched into my favourite topic, the Nikimoto Pine, only four inches tall but delivers a full crop of titchy little cones every October, he suddenly put his hand over mine and said I had these really lovely eyes, they sort of lit up when I got enthusiastic.

I do not know which way to turn. Obviously, I would rather he was a woman, I would leave Yvonne like a shot, but you cannot wait all your life for a girl with an interest in little oriental flora to come along, I am 42 next birthday. What should I do?

Yours etc

Willow, Tit Willow, Tit Willow

Given that the Pakistani bowlers did rather better with the ball which replaced the one they were rumoured to have tampered with, it is now clear that the cheating without which they could not possibly have beaten the greatest cricket team the world has ever seen must have been deployed elsewhere. I have therefore re-run my Test match videos and am in a position to reveal a scandal even more heinous and damning than any hitherto mooted.

It is patently obvious to me that the Pakistanis somehow managed to tamper with England's bats. Time and time again, balls from Waqar Younis and Wasim Aqram, often delivered at hardly more than 200 mph and rarely swinging through more than 30 degrees, either went straight through or straight past the English willow, or were snicked off outside edges to result in dolly slip catches any British schoolgirl could have held. Quite how these concealed holes could have been drilled into our brave lads' bats, or how those devilish edges could have been either glued on or planed off, I am not yet in a position to say, but be assured I shall not let the matter rest.

Fayre Game

Unable to decide which traditional Easter festivals to visit tomorrow? Fret no longer: here is my brief selection of the best:

Nolesbury Pus Fayre, Nolesbury, Lincolnshire. Marks the bursting of Edward II's neck-wen, 1318. Traditional crafts and contests – gypsy boil-letting, knobbly blackhead competition, Pimply Queen parade, greasy carbuncle contest, etc. Starts 10 am, Acne Yard.

Ffinchingham Stockbroker Trials, Ffinchingham, Bucks. Village weekenders in various initiative tests: Identify-a-Cow, Fifty-Yard-Hike, Dust-the-Range-Rover, Pull-on-the-Green-Wellie, Low-Beam-Headminding, Shut-the-Bloody-Gate, Avoid-Stepping-in-that, etc. Female visitors not admitted without Hermès scarf. Mulled Perrier.

Vintage Wheelie-Bin Rally, Brighton. Hundreds of valuable prizes, sheep-kissing, nude grocery, Sir Isaiah Berlin Lookalike Contest, melon juggling (Sussex constabulary vs Flat Earth Society Juniors). Starts 9 am, The Old Denture Exchange, Hove. (*No pacifists.*)

Lambert Newton Virgin Rolling, Lambert Newton, Hunts. Basically a crude form of football, the Virgin Rolling involves two teams of male villagers, 30 per side, who, according to rules drawn up by Henry III, 'muste rol a Virginne of ye parishe either to Northe Gaite or to Southe Gaite & not interfear wyth hir until one gait or other has been gayned.' In modern times, of course, the rules have been modified: the disappearance of virgins has meant that Mrs Rene Wentworth's standing offer is annually taken up, forcing an increase in the teams to 40 a side.

Fat Chance

Monday's news that US women were rebelling against the slimming industry by declaring that fat was now the thing to be will have come as no surprise to lovely obese Samantha Charnley of Romford, who has just won the coveted Weightseekers' Fat Lump of the Year Award.

'You wouldn't believe it to see me now,' she told me when I phoned to congratulate her, 'but I was once a disgusting seven stone. I'd put on a size 28 frock from somewhere smart like Huge Her Modes, and it would just hang on me. I'd sit there in the changing cubicle sobbing, watching through the curtains while enormous customers primped about in their trendy new clothes and brought the plaster off the walls. But then I pulled myself together: you've got to do something about your weight, Samantha, I said, or your husband will have no more relations with you.'

So she started buying *Fatter's Weekly* and following its diets assiduously. 'I had this craving for lemon juice and Philadelphia Light, but I learned to beat it. Some nights I would shift 40 lbs of chips. I do not know what I would have done without my friend Sharon from Slimmers Anonymous, many's the time she gave up her evenings to shovel bread pudding into me after I was too tired to lift my spoon, and where would I be without my husband Norm? He has been a pillar of strength, turning over his weekends to making porridge and filling me with Guinness.'

But, finally, her perseverance paid off. Yesterday, she received Weightseekers' handsome Bronze Pig for getting her weight up to a shapely 29 stone. 'I can't get into any of my old clothes now,' she told reporters happily, 'I've thrown away all my bikinis and bought a lovely German tent in blue and orange with a little window in the back so's Norman can climb in. Needless to say, our relations have perked up no end.'

In addition to the prestigious award, Samantha also wins a fabulous eating fortnight for two at a Bavarian McDonald's, the strengthened floor of her dreams from the Wembley Joist Company, a Mappin and Webb EPNS dinner-shovel, three seats for the Wimbledon Men's Final, and a freezerful of suet worth almost £40.

Storm Warnings

As soon as Hurricane Andrew finally blew itself out, after a typically boisterous, noisy and totally irresponsible spree in which an incalculable amount of expensive damage was done to everything it touched and something like four billion bread rolls were thrown about, I rang the United States Weather Bureau to inquire what the rest of the tempest season had in store, now that their nomenclature system had been established.

They told me that while Hurricane Anne, due any minute, was expected to be nothing but a spasmodic series of short chilly blasts likely to do little more than leave icicles on anything unwisely exposed, Hurricane Charles, which comes next, would be an altogether more threatening proposition. Seriously wet and terribly windy, it would almost certainly knock down any modern architecture in its path, and plans are already in hand to evacuate families thus threatened into old buildings, however derelict, inconvenient or ugly, since these were bound to be spared. Similarly, since trees, flowers, shrubs,

vegetables and so forth would survive unscathed, human beings would be wise to position themselves as close to these as possible, especially if they were prepared to engage them in pleasant conversation until the storm had passed. The safest place of all would be in the middle of a polo field.

Hurricane Charles, I understand, will be followed, slowly and miserably, by Hurricane Di, a bout of prolonged drizzle and low moaning winds in

which damage to designer frocks and hairstyling will be described as 'real torture'. Walkmans may be snatched off by sudden angry gusts, and anyone feeling unstable will run a serious risk of being blown downstairs or into the furniture.

Thankfully, though, this will soon peter out to make way for Hurricane Edward, an altogether gentler phenomenon unlikely to do anything worse than bring roses to the cheeks, though this cannot, unfortunately,

be said for the last in this season's sequence, which could well be the wildest and most devastating of all.

Hurricane Fergie is expected to wreak unimaginable havoc, involving countless millions in compensation, striking exclusive holiday resorts all over the world, fatally blowing thousands of brave photographers out of trees, and leaving all those unfortunate enough to be caught in its path without even the clothes they stand up in.

A Winkle Writes

Dear Sir,

Were you as outraged as I was by the Ministry of Agfish announcement that the giant Japanese whelk had arrived on our shores? I doubt it: how could you be, you have only seen newspaper photographs, you probably said to yourself, hallo, a whelk the size of a cauliflower, I could go for that, never mind a pin, bring me a crowbar, it is not just a dinner, either, when I have finished I could put my head inside it and hear the sea, it will be a whole new entertainment experience, if the BBC has got any sense it will put it on instead of *Eldorado*.

You say all that because you have not seen it for real, you have not been down here at the sharp end, you have not considered the ramifications.

This is a superwhelk. Not only is it twenty times the size of an English whelk, English whelks are what it feeds off to get that big, also English mussels, oysters, and, God help us, winkles. It has got this huge proboscis it pokes into our shells and sucks us out through, we do not have an answer, we have been caught napping, we are overwhelmed, it is Pearl Harbor all over again.

Worse, it is also Nipponese technology all over again. Even looking at just a photo, you must have clocked that it is an exact copy of an English whelk, only bigger. The Japs have said to theirselves, people over there must be sick and tired of spending all day trying to prise a square meal out of a pint of molluscs, never mind getting half of it down their tie, why don't we give them something they can eat with a knife and fork, also a nice ashtray at the end of it, or, for the musically inclined, drill a hole in one end, you can play *O Mine Papa*?

It is the same old story. Ask anyone in the motor industry. Try and find an English camera. What's your radio called? Who built your calculator?

If this goes on, Englishmen will soon find theirselves sitting down of a Sunday to roast whelk, Tokyo pudding and Nissan sprouts. What I want to know is where is John Selwyn Gummer? He ought to be out there off Broadstairs with his trousers rolled up to the knee and a knotted Union Jack on his head, lashing out with a coke hammer for Queen and country. That is what leadership means.

Yours etc

A Little Learning

Like you, I was outraged by Scotland Yard's attempt to destroy this great nation's already threatened education system by recommending the removal from the High Street of educational videos.

Almost everything that has ever been of any use to me I have learned by the simple expedient of coughing up a couple of pounds. I am, for example, an expert with both the chain-saw and the bull-whip, I could, in an emergency, remove a human brain without costly anaesthetic, employing only the contents of an ordinary kitchen drawer. I could cook a tasty meal for six people using nothing more than the materials you would find lying around in the average cemetery, I would humbly describe myself as an expert when it comes to animal husbandry, and I am fully qualified to run a women's prison, even one suddenly struck by a shortage of uniforms.

God alone knows what the police force thinks it's up to, but let us at least attempt to find a bright side to look on. Since I have learned most of what I know from the highly instructive videos shown at section house stag nights, perhaps we should assume that all this is simply the Met's somewhat ham-fisted attempt to clear the High Street shelves of old stock to allow our invaluable educational establishments to make room for new stuff.

A Scholar Writes

Dear Sir,

I recently got 38 GCSEs, but I decided not to stay on at school because they sent me a wossname to fill up about going into something called the Vith Form, and I do not want to do Vith, I do not even know where they speak it, so I decided to go for a job because everyone said with my qualifications I could walk into anything, but what I walked into was the door due to where it was not automatic like you get at Tesco's, it had this funny little knob thing, how was I to know, I did not do GCSE Knob. Then this man came out and picked me up and said have you broken anything and I said, yes, a clock, in 1989, it is now stuck with the big hand on the one like a swan and the little hand on the one like a golf club, I think it's half past 14, and he said no, no, no, what I meant was should we get a doctor to look at you, you might have internal bleeding, and I said internal bleeding what? So he sort of stared at me for a bit and then he said have you got an appointment, so I showed him this letter they'd sent me and he said could I read it on account of he didn't have his glasses with him, and I said *read* it? What do you mean read it, they have done it in joined-up writing, who do you think I am, Winston Einstein, I can only read stuff what has come off of a food processor, so the man said, all right, just go up to the 15th floor.

Blimey, I mean, that is A-Level stuff, am I right, 15, so I got in the lift and I took my shoes and socks off and I'd managed to count as far as 13 when the door opened, but I got out anyway and this girl said if you're looking for personnel turn left, and I said bloody hell, do you think I have got a degree in geography, left could be anywhere, so she pointed and I went over to this door and it had KNOCK & ENTER written on it in nice big block capitals you could read, so I went in and there was these two men sitting at desks and I said Good morning, which of you is Mr Knock, and one said I beg your pardon, and after we rabbited for a bit the other one, it could've been Enter, he didn't say, told me he didn't think I was suitable, so I assume it is the same old story again, I am over-qualified, right?

Yours etc

Just for Openers

Hearing of the Medical Defence Union's concern over the number of instruments found inside patients after operations, I was intrigued by the following case report, sent to me by a patient who recently had it removed from his stomach.

HOROLOGICAL FINDINGS DURING POINTLESS TREATMENT OF POLYARTERITIS NODOSA BY SURGERY.

A 60-year-old woman was admitted to the Royal Wessex Hospital with abdominal pain. She had a six-month history of diffuse arthralgia, weight loss, intermittent fever, vomiting, and chiming every hour on the hour. She had been treated with prednisolone 30mg daily, but her distress had not diminished. She continued to chime, and was admitted for surgery.

An incision having been made in the intestinal tract, the patient was discovered not to be suffering from polyarteritis nodosa, as had been suspected, but from a gold self-winding pocket watch. Upon examination, the engraving revealed it to be the property of a consultant at the East Middlesex Hospital, who not only identified the watch but was also able to specify the exact time the obstruction had entered the patient, since it was the day on which the Rat & Cockle had closed early due to unacceptable singing in the snug, and he had returned to the theatre only half an hour late. Having lost his spectacles in a hernia patient the day before, he had failed to notice when the watch fell from his gown pocket into the open woman, who had been admitted with suspected peritonitis. This, however, proved to be nothing worse than a half-finished bootee dropped six months before by an anaesthetist at South Acton General, where the woman had been admitted for the removal of a gallstone which in fact turned out to be a Ronson lighter lost by the patient's gynaecologist two years earlier.

Surgical complications ensued when the East Middlesex surgeon requested the return of his gold watch. The Royal Wessex consultant maintained that finders constituted keepers, whereupon his registrar pointed out that he had spotted the watch in the first place. The argument became heated, and in order to put a rapid end to the matter, it was decided to finish the operation quickly and telephone a solicitor to arbitrate upon the ownership. The patient was sewn up and returned to the ward. Two hours later, the registrar discovered that his Thermos flask was missing.

Autumn: a Practical Checklist

A is for autumn, season of mists and mellow fruitfulness, ie bronchitis and stepping on rotten pears. This has been a wonderful summer for fruit — 18 million surplus tons of the stuff. You cannot answer the door in case it is another neighbour with a boxful of Cox's Orange Waspnests he is trying to offload. The only solution is to keep a crate of your own festering bruises by the front door and, as soon as the bell rings, thrust it generously into the arriving arms.

B is for bleeding radiators, a cry that penetrates the small hours of autumn as householders wake in a muck sweat to the bong and creak of newly switched-on heating systems. The householder then has to crawl around his premises, bleeding the individual radiators in order to silence them. This is a simple process in which, just by breaking your fingernails, you are able to receive a chestful of dirty boiling water.

C is for cold-starting. Summer's warmth may have encouraged us to believe we had a decent battery, but come the dank autumn, mornings echo to the hurr-hurr-hurr of sluggish fly-wheels, which is Nature's way of telling us it is time to drop an old battery on our foot.

D is for dahlias. Now is the time to lift the wet tubers, wrap them carefully in newspaper, and store them at the back of the garage so the frost will not get them. The frost will not get them because — once you have fitted your new battery — you will immediately back into the garage and flatten them.

E is for Esperanto, the language of universal understanding, in which the word for autumn is *Soddit*. It is universally understood.

F is for fungus. This is found in late autumn all over everything stored at the back of garages, if you did not run over the wet tubers in time.

G is for glazing. The onset of autumn is the moment when you suddenly realize that you have a number of missing panes which were not worth replacing during the summer, cricket balls and waving hoes being what they are, and that it is now time to measure up the frames, pop round to the glaziers, and come back with several panes of glass .05mm too wide. It is simplicity itself to widen the frames with a chisel, so that your new panes of glass are now .05mm too narrow.

H is for hormone powder, which you will need for dipping geranium cuttings in. Using a sharp Stanley knife, remove part of your thumb and dip the cuttings into the powder. This will nourish them so that when potted out and placed on a dry shelf in the greenhouse, they will be strong enough to withstand the frost whipping in through the .05mm gaps in your new panes for 10 minutes longer than undipped cuttings.

I is for going back to Trinidad damn quick, man. This is the standard reply of bus conductors asked for their opinion of the first cold snap.

J is for judo, one of the many courses now on offer as the new night-school classes begin up and down the country. It is also the most popular, since those mastering it will have the best chance of getting home from night school unmugged.

K is for *kyrie eleison*, the first words of the Mass, now being heard by congregants as they flock into churches to pray for their batteries, dahlias, windows, geraniums, etc. Others flock in because it is warmer than the houses where their central heating has failed to come on. Fights often break out between them and plumbers coming to confession.

L is for lawnmower. Now is the moment to ring up the service agents to give them plenty of time to say: 'Stone me, bloody hell, you must be joking, pull this one.' Do not worry: just dismantle the mower yourself, lay out all the components in sequence, following the manual's instructions for greasing and honing, and prepare to reassemble. *Now* worry.

M is for migration. Since ornithology began, no one has understood what makes birds suddenly decide to leave our shores. How do they *know* about flat batteries and burst pipes and party conferences?

N is for nose, the upper orifice of the respiratory tract. It is divided by a septum of cartilage, with nostrils which have a stiff growth of marginal hair to prevent the entry of foreign bodies. The nasal cavity is lined with mucous membrane which warms and moistens the air and ejects dirt. Inside the nose, three wide sacs, separated by plates of bone, lead back to the nasopharynx. The lining of the lower cavity is covered with cilia, the lining of the upper has olfactory cells which receive impressions of smell from entering particles and transmit them through a highly sophisticated nerve system to the brain. How, in autumn, a smart thing like that can suddenly pack up completely is an utter mystery.

O is for oysters, which can be eaten only from September to April. If they had the sense to hibernate, the bottom would drop out of the Tabasco market.

P is for party conferences. How they came to be held in a season traditionally associated with fog, gloom, decline, dampness and, above all, rot, is anybody's guess.

Q is for quiz, an endemic affliction which lies dormant during summer but which suddenly and virulently appears, like many other diseases, in autumn, often striking dozens of TV presenters simultaneously as new strains are introduced. Quiz is hideous, characterized in the sufferers by a dreadful rictus, glazed eyes, a hollow laugh, and saying the same catch-phrases over and over again. Even for non-sufferers, the sight of quiz can cause severe retching.

R is for roof conversion. As the name implies, this is a religious belief, based on the irrational conviction that the two cowboys who built you a snug cedarette granny flat in June will still be in business in September when the extension begins slowly sliding down the roof. There is little you can do except wait for it to fall into the garden; if it is not too damaged, you could always keep undemanding chickens in it.

S is for school, reminding us that a new academic year has begun and the poor blighters will have to drag themselves back from a long holiday to the misery of boring lessons, inedible food, worthless exams, bullying, and a future that seems to hold no hope. Their pupils go back, too.

T is for tortoise, a sort of large oyster which *does* have the sense to hibernate, though not the sense to do it in the snug cardboard premises you have so lovingly prepared. You thus have all the fun of rooting about in your autumn mud patch, trying to find it, and the further fun, having found it, of deciding whether it has already hibernated, or is just dead.

U is for ultra-violet lamps, which you should now switch on and sit under to maintain that fading holiday tan. Leave it any later, and the burns won't heal in time for your next holiday.

V is for vivisection. This is another way of determining whether your tortoise is alive or dead; though if the latter, then it of course becomes mortisection. Either way, once you have carried it out, the point in doing it will have become academic. Particularly to the tortoise.

W is for winter, which is what autumn is for those prepared to call a spade a spade. Those prepared to call a spade a bloody waste of time will be anyone who has just come back with his new battery and run over the dahlias. Those prepared to call everything a bloody waste of time will be anyone who has just come back with his new battery and run over the dahlias *and* the tortoise.

X is for Xmas, which starts in early autumn, except during a recession, when it starts in late summer. Those wishing to know if there is a recession should check their local shop windows for cotton wool. Unlike Kenneth Clarke, cotton wool gives you a straight answer.

Y is for Youth Opportunities Programme, commemorated each autumn on 5 November when the young are allowed to earn a few pennies in return for supporting the idea that opponents of the Government should be burned alive. There is no alternative.

Z zzz is the noise made by a tortoise which enables you to determine whether it is alive or dead. Unfortunately, it happens only in cartoons.

Money in the Bank

Hearing that our wonderful but tragically hard-pressed High Street banks may be forced to reintroduce charges for those in credit, thousands of devoted customers have written to me asking how they can help. Do they, runs their most frequent question, have to be seriously in credit, or will their bank accept money from them even if they have only a bob or two?

Yes, of course. As one caring manager told me, were a widow, say, to have nothing more than a mite in her current account, the bank would gladly take it off her. Indeed, far-reaching and imaginative plans are now in hand to levy a whole range of exciting new charges hitherto undreamt of, to enable each and every one of us to rally to the banks in their hour of need and thus express our gratitude for the fact that when it was we who needed them, they were always so eager to help.

Take, for example, the proposed door-levy. Soon, whenever you open your bank's door, a little bell will tinkle, indicating that a fiver has been automatically debited from your account to go towards the wear and tear on the hinges, scuffing to the carpet you are about to

walk on, and damage to the Next Counter sign which was slapped sharply down on the only free window the moment you entered.

Which brings me to the queueing charge. The banks quite reasonably argue that if you were not standing about for hours on their premises, you would be out there in the rain, throwing money away in shops, running the risk of being knocked down by a bus, and so on. It is thus only fair that you should be asked to chip in for

warmth and shelter. So too with the Social Charge, soon to be levied in return for access to a counter hand prepared to talk to you through the little holes in her armoured glass. As the banks rightly point out, this would cost you 48p a minute on any chatline, and you wouldn't even be able to see the girl, let alone have her humiliate you in front of a lot of other people, a service for which many a television personality would willingly cough up 80 quid.

These are just a few of the services soon to be available. The full list is shown on a leaflet you will be able to pick up at your local branch, for less than a tenner. Should you, by the way, wish by any remote chance not to give your bank any money but instead to borrow some, the correct form of words is: 'My name is Morris Maxwell, I am a long-lost brother and I have a fabulous scheme for turning water into wine, all I need is £400,000,000 in used notes.'

A Sheikh Writes

Dear Effendi,

I write to express my outrage at the appalling actions of your repugnant profession in hounding Mr David Mellor out of office.

My close friend Mr Mellor (or David, as I had been expecting to be able to call him very soon) was supposed to be coming out here for Christmas, together with his wife, his children, his daily and her parents, several uncles and their families, a close friend of his barber, and the people from up the road, together with their elderly gardener, who, I am

told, is a vegetarian and also needs a special bed, due to a hernia. I have thus made copious arrangements, all of which will now come to nothing.

You will say, oh, he is a rich Arab, he can easily write off 63 Concorde tickets, he probably needed to redecorate the palace anyway, what is an extra tennis-court here or there, but you do not know the half of it. Since Muslims do not celebrate Christmas, what am I to do with this 90-foot tree from Norway, I have two men

watering it round the clock, what about the ten gross of glass balls and little lights, never mind the Bing Crosby fairy on the top, specially commissioned from Aspreys, which sings 'White Christmas'

and throws gift-wrapped Rolex Oysters at my esteemed house-guests, what about the twenty

turkeys running around all over the place eating threepenny bits, also two hundredweight of Brussels sprouts, one hundred funny hats, and a tankerful of advokaat, what is to become of all this?

I look to you tabloid people to make amends for the damage you have caused. I understand you remain in constant touch with the Duchess of York; please inform me if she has firmed up her Yuletide plans yet.

Yours etc

A Half-crown Writes

Dear Sir,

May I crave the indulgence of your esteemed columns to reassure millions of loyal British subjects of Her Gracious Majesty (whose radiant face I am honoured to wear on my back) that my former colleague the florin will not, as some irresponsible newspapers have suggested, disappear forever.

It will not be dumped off Heligoland, it will not be melted down for scrap, it will not be turned into naff cufflinks and medallions; it will, as the last of the old pre-decimal servants of our proud island race, be relocated down here in The Bide-A-Wee Home for Imperial Coinage. It will be happy here. It will have the time of its life.

It will be reunited with all its mates from the good old days when it could go down to Brighton, buy a slap-up fish dinner, a pint of

Watney's, a packet of Woodbines, and still give fourpence change. There are millions of us here now: the Tanners are next door to me, the Shillings are across the corridor, the Pennies, the Halfpennies and the Farthings are all upstairs in the Copper Suite, and the Threepenny Bits have got their own little room in the attic.

Hallo, I hear your readers saying, this is a bit bloody peculiar, what is the point of hanging on to all that old junk? Yes, well, it just shows you how little most people know about fiscal policy, they think Kenneth Clarke is just two pretty faces, they do not know what he has got up his sleeve in the event of the Bundesboche, as he calls it,

getting up to its old tricks again. He was down here only last week on Chancellor's Inspection, wasn't he, checking on the stock etcetera, doing his sums on the back of his special envelope. He has got this master plan in the event of Britain being forced to go it alone. Never mind your ERM, never mind your single currencies, never mind your floating pound. He will play his imperial card: we shall be back to pounds, shillings and pence before Jerry knows what's hit him. I should like to see the D-mark cope with £4.7s.3¾d., I should like to see hot-shot teenage currency speculators trying to second-guess the groat, they will blow all their terminals, they will be up to their braces in smoke, there will not be a computer left standing between Calais and the Urals!

Yours etc

To Hell in a Handcart

Faced with the fact that there are now almost 10,000 supermarket trolley accidents a year — *more than 90 per cent involving women!* — the Health and Safety Executive has issued safety guidelines for driving these highly dangerous vehicles. But though I personally forked out £4 for the snappy little HMSO publication, I could find no mention therein of the root cause of this latest Nineties urban curse. It is, of course, that old friend of ours, unemployment.

Trolley-hotting is directly attributable to housewives' boredom, brought on by the supermarkets themselves for selling so many items designed to reduce household labour, from nine-course pre-cooked microwave banquets to aerosol cleaners capable of polishing an entire four-bedroomed house with just one quick squirt.

In consequence, unemployed housewives now have so much time on their hands that they have clearly taken to descending

gang-handed on Tesco's, Safeway, and the rest, grabbing unattended high-performance trolleys, and racing them up and down the aisles with inevitably dreadful consequences. Remember, many of these joyriders may never have handled anything trickier than a string bag or a little tartan pull-along wheelie. What, then, is to be done? It is no use trolley-manufacturers racking their brains for refinements designed to thwart the hotters, the problem must

be tackled at its socio-economic roots.

It is essential that work be found for these unfortunate victims of the times we live in, and the sooner enlightened legislation is put in place to ensure the return of the labour-consuming kitchen, the podded pea, the undisposable nappy, the washboard, the tin bath, the feathered chicken, the scrubbing brush, the mangle, and the oven-unready non-chipped potato, the better it will be for everyone.

Red Squares

Intrigued to read that Moscow is now seeking to attract tourists by promoting its night life, I couldn't resist writing off for a brochure.

ON THE TOWN

'See you later, crocodile!' This is cry you are hearing at every turn in downtown Moskva when sun sets and anything is going! Feet tap, fingers snap, and people shout: 'Who is that crazy hepcat?' as some famous face from wireless or Agronomy Advisers Relocation Department goes ape and sashays to the mean beat of the GUM Trouser Counter Hot Five, currently rocking them at the Vishinsky Banqueting Rooms, where the elite meet. Entry is costing only ten roubles, to include first jug wodke and slap-up two-course Beetroot Dinner. Gals five roubles if unaccompanied.

Or why not drop in to new nitespot Chicago Brian's, where your genial host has reconstructed complete atmosphere of Rolling Twenties? Top posh clientele is drinking bathtub coffee out of gin bottles, there is tombola where you can win big, big prizes such as imported lightbulbs, and dancers go Latin-American to the rhythms of El Capone's Sambo Band. Men must wear shirt. Ring 667583 for table reservations, six months' waiting list.

Afterwards, who is for stroll to Niv Lorry Show-rooms? Here, the new 18-tonner turns under spotlight, and all clap. 'Hit me again, daddy!' shout the in-crowd. New on the Strip is Nikolai, Man of a Thousand Noises. Nikolai just blew in from trendy Kiev, where he has been playing to packed canteens. With-it guys and dolls can catch his act at the corner of Oznayov Prospekt and Lumumba Alley. Throw him a kopeck and he will imitate Rover the Dog, Humphrey Cagney, train getting up steam, you name it! Is also escaping (sometimes) from sack.

But what is really setting this wacky town alight is new Playboy Disco Whisky-a-Gogo Topless Singles Bar! Rabbit Girls come to your table with their famous dip (garlic curry eaten with thumb) while on the stage, Uzbekhs take their vests off. A big radiogram with nearly seven of the latest Ruby Murray pressings provides that sensational Toytown beat, and every lady gets a bar of carbolic soap to take home, with the compliments of your swinging host, Dick Putz. Our kind of guy!

All Change

As a devout monarchist, I was deeply touched to learn from an authoritative Palace source that, as a concession to demands for the Royal Family to reduce its burden on those who actually do pay taxes, Her Majesty the Queen has graciously agreed to major economies on the Royal Train.

From 1 November, there will be no dining-car between London and Sandringham, except on Mondays and Thursdays. Senior members of the Royal Family will, however, be able to obtain hot snacks from the buffet,

The next train's in ten minutes Ma'm, but there won't be another Royal one till Thursday

while minor Royals will find an adequate supply of crisps, peanuts and cold drinks (except Tango on Fridays and Sundays) from the vending machine (change given).

There will also be a reduced service to Windsor: on Tuesdays and Saturdays, it will terminate at Reading, whence the family will continue by Royal Bus, and from January to April only royal pensioners will be able to take advantage of the new Royal Awayday; members under 65 (60 in the case of princesses) will pay full fare, unless accompanying a corgi on official duties.

In future, the sleeper to and from Sandringham will not provide a cooked breakfast; there will, however, be complimentary tea-making facilities and a biscuit (not chocolate, unless the premium of 10p has been paid, in advance, to the steward) in all compartments (except weekends), and the bar will stay open (Queen Mothers only) as far as Carlisle. Royal Bicycles may continue to be carried in the guard's van provided that (a) prior arrangement has been made in writing, and (b) cheques have been given three full working days to clear.

Absolutely Barking

I have to tell you that I wholeheartedly concur in the Princess Royal's support for the practice of docking the tails of working dogs so that they may better perform the duties that man requires of them. I myself have had a working dog for many years, and, with the caring help of an accommodating veterinary surgeon, have introduced a number of alterations which have made all the difference to our life together. For example, sympathizing with the great difficulty the poor creature had in bringing back from my newsagent the several papers I daily order, I immediately arranged, at considerable personal expense, to have his mouth widened to accommodate not only newspapers and magazines, but also boxes of typing paper, cartons of cigarettes, and bottles of Tizer.

However, though this further eased his burden when engaged upon his evening task of fetching my pipe and slippers, he still had trouble with my dressing-gown, the weight of which bent his back most severely. I therefore saw it as my caring duty to ask the vet to graft on an extra pair of legs to support the creature's middle, for which, I know, he was enormously

thankful, since it also increased his ability to scratch by 50 per cent, well worth the thrashing he regularly received from bringing so many more muddy footprints into the house after going outside to fetch in the coal on the delightful little cart I had bolted to his hindquarters. And lest you think that cruel, let me quickly say that it was unbolted for meals, which he took standing at the table (to save me the inconvenience of bending down), shovelling the food into his enormous mouth with the convenient little hand which the vet had removed from a chimpanzee whose owner had objected to the way it picked its nose.

My dog is watching me even as I write. Soon, he knows, it will be time for him to take my copy to the *Sunday Express*, skilfully negotiating the London traffic on his six tiny skates. Man's best friend, indeed!

You Cannot Be Sirius!

You will be thrilled to learn that I have just received a telephone call from Smiley, the newly discovered tenth planet of our solar system whose photograph (and a very good likeness, too) you will all have seen in Wednesday's newspapers.

It was a somewhat crackly line, which I originally attributed to the fact that Smiley is 3,700,000,000 miles away, until corrected by my caller who informed me that the hitherto exemplary telephone system had recently been privatized, since when they had had no end of trouble. He had also, that very minute, opened a gas bill for 9 million laffs, roughly the cost of a new ring road, which had given his address as 24 Acacia Crescent, Pluto. I told him that it was a funny old world, and he replied that I did not know the half of it, the reason he knew the price of a ring road was because they had just had one built around the capital, Joke, and the traffic-jam had been solid for six weeks. To make matters worse, the laff, as the result of an unprecedented governmental U-turn, had just been allowed to float against the Uranian conker, which for some reason had had the immediate effect of plunging the economy into even more dire economic straits. This was completely beyond him, all he knew was that he now owed 9,000 conkers on a house worth only 400 laffs, where would it end, next thing you knew the banks would start making people bankrupt to ensure that borrowers would never be in a position to pay back the money they shouldn't have been lent in the first place, it would be like someone coming along to clamp your car to the road in order to make traffic flow more easily, wouldn't it?

The only bright spot of his week, he went on, was that his son had just passed 196 GCSEs, not bad for a lad with an IQ of 41, lucky they'd lowered standards a bit to make it easier for kids to get into the universities they were planning to close down so that not too many graduates would be released on to the shrinking job market, it all made sense to him, though he remained in two minds about shutting down hospitals to raise money to dig a tunnel to Venus, what did I think?

I said I wasn't in any real position to judge, and asked him why, though it was of course nice to hear from him, he had phoned me in the first place. He said that now Smiley had been discovered, everybody there was very keen to join the EC. They firmly believed, he said, that they had a lot to offer.

Spring in the Step

Tomorrow being yet another bank holiday, there could be no better time for a history-rich English country walk. May I suggest my own favourite, from Chester-le-Conklin to Norton-cum-Strangely?

Chester-le-Conklin (*pron.* Fargwick), in the high country of N Wilts, is chiefly famous for having once been represented by Lord Gryll, the shortest peer in England, who rode about on a bull terrier and, following the Virgin Riots of 1681, escaped to Holland disguised as a churn. The incident is recorded on a plaque in Dog Passage, where a statue was put up to the bull terrier, Hank, who represented the town at Westminster after his master's flight. The inscription reads: *To goodlie Hank, our trustie Member, never drunke and his mouth allways shutte, from the loyal folke of the town, 1687.*

At the S end of Dog Passage, where it joins Twinge Lane, former site of the old tooth museum, there is a fine view of St Bill's and its twin spires, which lean in opposite directions. The architect, Jethro Nuke, was later buried in quicklime; on Whit Monday, apprentices climb the two spires and throw a pumpkin from one to the other, representing the head of Nuke. In the evening, there are bonfires and dirty films.

From Chester-le-Conklin, take the road to Dung Magna, a hamlet long associated with Merlin, whose kidneys are supposed to be buried under Faerie Mound. There is a belief that on Midsummer Night the kidneys come out and dance on the village green; this is tricky to substantiate, now that Faerie Mound is the ground floor of Tesco's, but a friendly warehouseman may be persuaded, for a few pounds, to show you where the kidneys might have been before the loading bays were dug.

Walking NE from Dung Magna, you pass Tyler's Stump. Known as Tyler's Oak until it was felled in error in 1979 (the DoE chopped it down to see if it had Dutch Elm Disease), it is where Wat Tyler paused in 1381 on his way from Canterbury to Blackheath. Since it is 150 miles off any possible route from Canterbury to Blackheath, it is not difficult to see why he paused.

From here, it is but a short step to Norton-cum-Strangely and its famous Circle, a con-figuration of megalithic stones which have no relationship to one another; there is no Druidic significance in their numbers, and at sunrise, they make no meaningful, or even interesting, pattern. Nor does much mystery surround how they were dragged here, since geologists are agreed they came from about 12 yards away. The likeliest explanation so far advanced is that it was something built by drunks.

A Tailor Writes

Dear Sir,

Listen, I don't want to complain, recessions you have to live with, who said we were put on this earth to be happy, but tell me, you're a clever man, what have I done to deserve Lady Moon on top of everything else? A woman cuts four inches off the sleeves of all her husband's 32 wonderful hand-made Savile Row suits, and all of a sudden she's some kind of a heroine? I tell you, you look away for a minute, and the whole world goes mad.

What this will do to the tailoring trade is nobody's business. You think I'm joking? Nobody's business is exactly what we'll get, because who in his right mind is going to spend six, seven hundred pounds on a bespoke whistle when any minute some crazy woman can take it into her head to start doing alterations without a licence, just on account of he came home a little late and had his socks in his pocket?

Cheap off-the-peg is what men are going to buy, now. Rubbish from East Germany, Taiwan, you name it, places where they know nothing from basting, from inter-lining, from an invisible gusset you can let out if a man puts on a little weight. The media stick Lady Moon on some kind of a pedestal, suddenly men say to them-selves, all right, so it pinches a bit under the arms, so it rucks up a bit at the back, what can you expect for 80 quid, at least I'm not going to come home from the office party and find 10 grands worth of offcuts in the dustbin.

For two pins I'd sell up and drive a minicab, believe me. For *one* pin.

Yours etc

Ape of the Tarzans

You were doubtless astonished by Wednesday's news story concerning the Malaysian orang-utan who stripped a French tourist naked and ran off with all his clothes. I was not. It came as no surprise to me at all. I had long been expecting something of the sort.

In 1986, my old friend Lord Greystoke, who runs a rubber plantation out there, wrote to say that on one of his forays into the jungle he had come across an infant ape who had been abandoned by its parents. He brought the little fellow home, and so great a rapport developed between them that Greystoke, a bachelor, decided to bring it up as his own son. It was, he said, considerably more intelligent than most aristocratic offspring he had met, many of whom could not peel a banana without the assistance of a nanny.

Little Greystoke was sent home to Eton where he was an instant success, being anti-intellectual and enormously athletic; he had, furthermore, a way of looking at unpopular masters while bending a school railing between his bare hands that ensured an untroubled life for everyone in the class. He could also eat with his foot.

Sexually, he remained something of a mystery. Once a month he would go off to Whipsnade, and return looking happier, but, naturally, no one pressed him on the subject. They were all members of the English upper classes, and stranger things had happened, even in the best families.

Given all this, it was no surprise when, at the age of four, he was offered a commission in a good Guards regiment, since not only did his knuckles brush the ground more impressively than anyone

Young Greystoke could be the best player we ever had headmaster - if only we could find a way to teach him the rules

else's (with, of course, the exception of the Brigadier), his ability to communicate with the horses surpassed that of even the Royal Family. Furthermore, he single-handedly beat the Marines team at the Royal Tournament in the race to swing a 12-pounder over a wall by tucking the gun under his left arm and grasping the rope in his right. He was also a huge social success: at hunt balls, he could swing from chandeliers and lay out waiters with magnums of Bollinger hurled as easily as if they had been coconuts.

He tended, inevitably, to smell a bit when hot; in short, young Greystoke was everything that an officer and a gentleman should be. It is thus clear to me from Wednesday's news that he has returned to Malaysia to see his father; for, like any aristocrat, he never pays his tailor's bills, and, if his credit had been suspended and he needed a suit, then the Frenchman was an obvious source. Quite why he did need the suit, mind, is anyone's guess; mine is that, Michael Heseltine having spectacularly removed himself from the running, the ape intends to return to England to form a government. I very much hope I'm right.

Your Winter Queries Answered

Following this week's sudden cold snap, thousands of readers worried witless by, yet again, the seasonally unexpected, have written to me for advice. Since I can reply to only a few, I have chosen the most typical.

Dear Sir

For 15 years, I ran my own highly profitable light-engineering company employing 200 skilled operatives, but as the result of Norman Lamont's commitment to doing something for small businesses, I now play the spoons outside the Odeon, Leicester Square.

I had a reasonably successful summer season, going down particularly well with queues of Japanese light-engineering holidaymakers who had more money than they knew what to do with, but now that the cold weather is upon us I have found it impossible to play the spoons in gloves. I recently attempted to change my act by singing a medley from *Chu Chin Chow*, but a baritone ex-stockbroker working the Plaza queue opposite with selections from *South Pacific* ran across the square and broke my nose. If, as is rumoured, the Grimethorpe Colliery Brass Band arrives after the weekend, it will be all up with me. Is there anything you can suggest?
Sir Esmond Cattermole, Waterloo Bridge

Dear Sir Esmond, I have had many inquiries like yours, each more distressing than the one before; only last week, an elderly professor of Bantu Philology, whose department has been liquidated to help stabilize the pound, wrote to ask my advice on freeing a trombone slide which had been attacked by superglue vandals during his pitiful attempt on Tiger Rag outside the Oxford Woolworth's. There was nothing I could do to help.

In your case, I suggest that you give up music altogether and address the queues on the merits of the wonderful new BR fare increases. Though your tin cup will be ignored, your behaviour will almost certainly occasion a breach of the peace, and a night in a snug Bow Street cell plus hot breakfast to follow is not to be sneezed at.

Speaking as your nurse, Colonel, I'd say it was time to turn the heating on

Dear Sir

My husband Dudley and I are planning to have another try at a winter-sports holiday and desperately need your advice. Last October, we spent a very great deal of money learning to ski on the steel rollers at the Ruislip Indoor Ski School. In January, we laid out yet more money flying to St Moritz to put our learning to the test, having been assured that it was the very best time of year to go, weatherwise.

I have to tell you that we spent the entire two weeks in the hotel lounge, waiting for steel rollers to fall. Not one fell throughout the entire fortnight. Worse, the slopes were covered in some ghastly white muck which made walking virtually impossible. Is Swiss weather always like this? If not, when is the best time to go for really good steel rollers?
Daphne Hislop, Tring

Dear Mrs Hislop, I deeply sympathize. My own uncle, a patriot to his marrow, spent much of 1940 heroically grappling with a Link trainer, only to find at the end of it that the authorities expected him to suspend himself over Hamburg in some lunatic contraption while things were fired at him. He immediately became a conscientious objector and

died, a broken man, in Wilmslow.

I wish there were an easy answer to your inquiry, but knowing the Swiss as I do, I do not expect heavy falls of steel rollers until there is money in it

Dear Sir

Two years ago, I applied for a Lloyds Cashpoint card, not because I wanted to 'Obtain Up To £200 From Conveniently Located Dispensers Without Waiting' (as a matter of fact I have always liked waiting in banks, due to seeing a wide cross-section of humanity some of whom might one day be famous and then you could say I know him, he goes to my bank, he is actually shorter than he is on the wireless), but because I got a tip from a colleague on the Men's Toiletries Counter that a Cashpoint card was just the thing for scraping frost off your windscreen.

Due to said use pending two winters, however, friction has rubbed away some of the embossed numbers. I did not notice this, since I do not, as I say, use the card for its intended purpose, but eight months ago I found myself stranded without money in Wincanton and, much against my will, put the card into a Lloyds dispenser. Nothing happened, except a lot of red lights came on and a bell started ringing somewhere, after which I

was invited to step into the manager's office where two men in navy raincoats said: 'Charles Arthur Maurice Negley, we are arresting you for the Luton casino job, do not give us no trouble, son, we are tooled up and will not hesitate to use reasonable force.'

I explained to them about being someone else and the numbers on the card being rubbed off and obviously now forming the numbers of this person Negley, but was invited to pull this one on account of it had bells on. There was a similar response later up the Old Bailey, where I was informed that my story was the most preposterous farrago they had ever heard. I am now doing ten years for armed robbery, and do not know where to turn. What is your view of all this?
Esmond Tiptree, Parkhurst

**Dear Mr Tiptree,
My view of all this is that it is the most preposterous farrago I have ever heard.**

Dear Sir

My wife Hillary forgot to bring our tortoise in, and I think it could be dead. I have tried a few sharp cracks with a stick, but it didn't do no good. If this gets out, it could cost me the next election. What should I do?
B. Clinton, Washington

**Dear Mr Clinton,
Don't worry. Millions of people feel the same way as**

you about Hillary. Giving her a few sharp cracks with a stick could swing several states your way.

Dear Sir

As a matter of principle, I do not put my overcoat on until 10 October. It is my view that one of the reasons this country is going to the dogs is that people are getting soft; if you have to be a pansy to get your own television show, I would rather stay in surgical sundries, thank you very much, even if it means you cannot use the company Lada at weekends.

However, surgical sundries means walking across a lot of forecourts, up paths, and so forth, and when the cold snap comes, an overcoat is essential. But this year, when I put it on, having hung on the peg since 31 May (the overcoat, not me), I not only got a weird sensation when inserting my hand in the outside pocket, I also noticed that all three of our plaster ducks went wonky, including the largest which is held on by not one but two hooks. This carried on all week, by the end of which, especially as I also wound my hat up in the Lada window and trod in something in Palmers Green, I was convinced there was a poltergeist in the pocket. What I want to know is, can you have an overcoat exorcized?
Chas. Neems (Mr), Sutton

**Dear Mr Neems,
Yes, there is no problem when it comes to removing evil spirits from an overcoat, but do have the hat done at the same time, because most priests will offer a discount on two items. The Yellow Pages are your best bet.**

Dear Sir

In all the countless billions of little snowflakes that have fallen since time began, no two have ever been alike! Do you not, like me, find this clear evidence of the Almighty's wondrous powers absolutely thrilling?
Kylie Rees-Mogg, Wembley

**Dear Ms Rees-Mogg,
Since you ask, I find it intensely depressing. If, after all these years, God still cannot get even the basic design of something as simple as a snowflake right, what hope has He got when it comes to something really tricky, like the Docklands Light Railway?**

As a matter of fact, I would dispute your evidence anyhow, since there is no way of comparing one snowflake with another. When two land on your sleeve, by the time you have studied the pattern of one, the other one has disappeared. This may of course simply be God's way of covering up His enormous embarrassment at the whole thing, but however you slice it, I see scant grounds for confidence.

A Canary Writes

Dear Sir,

Not only have I had it up to here with this government, I have had it up to here with your bloody colleagues, pardon my French, in Fleet Street, if that's where it is, I wouldn't know, I have never flown over anything, I do not even know if I can fly, I have never been given the opportunity to have a go, I have been stuck down a coalmine all my working life, you do not want to fly about down there, you'd get filthy.

Which brings me to my point. In all the millions of words written about pit-closures, in all the miles of bleeding-heart footage on the box, there has not been one single mention of canaries. What about us?

I also have been slung out on my ear, remember, or would have been if I had one, after a lifetime up the sharp end.

Never mind bloody miners, they have had it with jam on thanks to canaries, anyone notice a funny smell, send in the canary, anyone feeling a bit Uncle Dick,

where's that bird, catch my drift?

All them marchers last Wednesday, all them placards, did anyone shout 'Sack Major Not Joey!', did they hell, did anyone wave a banner saying 'Who's An Unemployed Boy, Then?', did Heseltine stand up in the House and say, 'Now, if I may come to canary policy. . .'

And not a word about retraining, neither. Shut the mines, and who needs a canary to go round sniffing

their premises for methane?

They want a canary who can run up a little ladder and ring a bell, they want a canary who can whistle 'Alexander's Ragtime Band', I have never been taught anything like that, my profession is sniffing, if I go down the Job Centre the first thing they'll ask is can you perch on someone's head without widdling, and I shall have to tell them it has never arisen, I have only perched on helmets, people don't mind what you do if they've got a helmet on, and God knows what you have to do to get the dole, I have not paid in any sunflower seeds over the years, nobody asked me to, I shall probably end up in the gutter taking pot luck with bloody sparrows and I do not even know how to go about that, I do not speak a word of Sparrow.

Please print this letter. Not that it'll do much good, mind, it will probably end up at the bottom of some jammy budgie bastard's cage like all your stuff.

Yours etc

Ground Control to Major John

I am delighted to see that experts have at last alerted us to the dreadful risks involved in the addiction to Virtual Reality. It has long been a source of deep astonishment to me that a system has been allowed to develop whose participants do not merely withdraw from real life into a hermetically sealed world, but, once there, do nothing but play games requiring them to come up with ever more preposterous solutions to problems entirely of their own making, none of this having any bearing whatever on what is going on in the world outside.

If I'd known they were going to do that, I'd never have voted for them in the first place.

Brief Encounter

My heart goes out to Network South-East commuters whose own will have sunk into their boots at the news that British Rail is introducing not only French water-cannons but also Swedish scrubbing machines which will operate in harness to remove leaves and other detritus from the region's rails.

I give it about ten minutes before blackboards start going up in London mainline stations illegibly explaining that the complete standstill of all services is unfortunately due to the completely unforeseen circumstances whereby, as the result of the wrong sort of water having been directed at the wrong sort of rails and hit the wrong sort of leaves, the Swedish scrubbing machines have not only become clogged solid with foliage, they have also, thanks to a totally unexpected cold snap involving the wrong sort of frost, been inseparably frozen to the French water-cannons.

Fiddling with the Knobs

With BBC rows and rumours this week reaching an unprecedentedly hysterical pitch, thousands of readers have naturally turned to me for the truth behind all this. Are BBC1 and BBC2 really to be merged, you ask, are Radios 1, 2 and 5 truly to be axed, will 5,000 more jobs indeed go, what is all this stuff about FM and long wave, is Director-General Birt about to get the bullet, does Culture Minister Peter Brooke know his arts from a hole in the ground? The truth is in fact even more exciting than all of that. John Birt and his chairman Marmaduke Hussey are in fact to be merged to form Duke Birt plc. This will operate from the attic formerly inhabited by Arthur Askey and Richard Murdoch atop Narrowcasting House, following the profitable conversion of all lower floors into the BeeBee Sauna-Pizza Reject Pottery Acid House Remaindered Bookstore and Used Car Garden Centre, and will commit itself to profit-responsible agglomerative transmission, or, more succinctly, PRAT.

This principle merges not only channels, but programmes, too. Thus, to pluck a few random examples from a leaked memorandum, I find that plans are already in hand for *Eldorama*, in which serious issues of the day will be discussed by out-of-work actors on a Spanish demolition site, *Points of Sportsnight*, in which Anne Robinson will read out postcards from viewers who want to know why there is no sport on, *That's Neighbours*!, in which Esther Rantzen will wave a selection of peculiarly shaped Australian vegetables, and *Mastermind 92*, in which Barry Norman will show the latest pictures of Magnus Magnusson, and ask himself questions about them.

Nor have radio listeners been forgotten. They will be catered for by a handsome full-colour wallchart from Duke Birt plc explaining how, simply by turning their TV set to face the wall, it will be just like the wireless. This wallchart will be given away, absolutely free, with every annual licence demand.

A Tortoise Writes

Dear Sir,

It is absolutely typical of the sod-you-Jack times we live in that nobody seems to give a toss about the Swift-Tuttle Comet. They all read in Monday's papers about this billion-ton chunk of ice currently belting towards Earth at 130,000 miles an hour, but as soon as they saw it wasn't due to collide with us until 14 August 2116, they all said, oh well, that's all right then, it will not affect house prices, it will not dent my Volvo, it will not frighten my cat, it will not interfere with my telly reception, I shall be well dead by then, and as I am being cremated I do not even have to worry about my tombstone being knocked wonky, what a relief!

Yes, well, thank you very much, but how about us tortoises? I shall be only 137 when this bloody thing strikes, I shall be hardly run in, I shall have a good couple of centuries left in me, but has Virginia Bottomley rung, has she hell, I have not got the first idea what to do come that 14 August, they will not even specify morning or afternoon, let alone what time. Do they have any inkling what it is like being a tortoise, we cannot just nip down the nearest Tube station when the sky starts filling up, we cannot nip anywhere, time we have got our head and feet inside it'll be all over. If they'd only tell us it'd be turning up at, for example, half-past five we could make a mental note to get going about two o'clock, at least we'd have time to get under a rock or similar.

And talking of timing, what a sensitive moment to break the news! I was just about to turn in for a good winter's kip. I shan't be able to get a bloody wink, now.

Yours etc

All Wrapped Up

With cottonwool snow already cascading down High Street windows, 'Jingle Bells' shrieking through supermarket loudspeakers, and ten thousand Santas flexing their laps to peak readiness in ten thousand grotti, it is once again time for the nation to begin driving itself barmy over the imminent need to start choosing Christmas presents.

Unless, that is, they are *Sunday Express* readers. For this newspaper, ever at the forefront of humanitarian concern, has commissioned an astonishingly revolutionary new product, the all-purpose Yuletide gift. Through a remarkable breakthrough in South Korean seasonal technology, we are able to offer, exclusive to our readership, the opportunity to solve all their gift problems at a single stroke with our incredible **DIGITAL AFTERSHAVE NECKTIE SLIPPERS!** These handsome plaid loafers in non-stick dishwasherproof Seoulene, a direct spin-off of the remarkable Korean space programme, are not just an example of head-turning footwear at its economical best. The left slipper has been micro-circuited and digitized to play up to 700 electronic games through the handy mini-screen built into its instep and activated by the big toe, while the right slipper contains nearly two pints of Old Phoo Yong Macho-Musk aftershave in its virtually imperceptible built-up heel*. A slim tube connects with the specially designed fashionable necktie, so that when the heel is brought down sharply, the face is automatically sprayed through the knot.

These items are a gift at only £59.95 a pair! Order before 8 December, and receive a handsome calculator-scarf with advokaat-scented bathcube woggle *ABSOLUTELY FREE*!

* Caution: a slight limp is inevitable. Sunday Express plc is not responsible for accidents or social embarrass-ment deriving therefrom.

Anything for a Few Sovs

I trust that, with the closure of Windsor Safari Park, a golden opportunity is not to be thoughtlessly thrown away. Since the main reason offered for its decline was that it was no longer of sufficient interest to families, it clearly cries out to be re-opened as the Windsor surely cannot be right, especially since Her Majesty's loyal subjects are forced to rely for their information about their gracious rulers upon those very sources, many of them, of course, notoriously unreliable.

Were, however, a number draw, from the close observation of this fascinating species, conclusions about their behavioural patterns, social techniques, mating habits, intelligence, the state of their various and peculiar pair-bondings, and much else besides. I for one would be a

Family Park. Stocked, of course, once the animals have been removed, with the Windsor Family.

For who could doubt that the main thing most people wish to do with these remarkable beasts is gawp at them? But hitherto, apart from the odd coronation, wedding, or similar formal and thus totally unrevealing occasion, this has been the almost exclusive privilege of hacks and paparazzi. That of gilded cages to be set up in the park, flood-lit and surrounded by terraced seating, visitors would flock by the coachload not merely to watch, say, the Duke of Edinburgh roaring, or the Prince and Princess of Wales throwing things at one another, or Prince Andrew swinging from his tyre, or the Princess Royal jumping up and down on the bonnet of a Land Rover, or the Duchess of York being fed, but also to fervent supporter of the Windsor Family Park. Not only would it benefit our beleaguered economy by attracting thousands of foreign tourists into the hard-currency purchase of enormous amounts of ice-cream, T-shirts, hamburgers, bumper-stickers, videos, baseball caps, souvenir ashtrays and individual fruit pies, it might also put the gutter Press out of business for good.

Littlestand

You will have read that the BBC is finding it ever-harder to compete in cable and satellite channels for major sporting events, and this will have depressed you no end, especially if you do not have a cable with a satellite on the end. But do not despair; I have written on your behalf to the Corporation, and received the following encouraging reply from Sir Marmaduke Birt, newly designated Head of Minor Sporting Events, in which he previews his exciting programme for next Saturday afternoon:

'There's not much about racing that Peter O'Sullevan doesn't know, Alan, and that's why he's running in the 2.15 at Shepherd's Bush next Saturday. In *Racing from TV Centre*, viewers will have the chance to see their favourite commentators in action, starting with the 1.30 Twice Round the Bar Handicap (.03 furlongs) in which novice chaser David Coleman will have his first outing following next Thursday's peak-time welterweight contest with Harry Carpenter.

'Immediately following the last race, viewers will go over to Wembley for the second leg of the UEFA Blow Football Cup, when, on the hallowed green tablecloth, Tottenham Notspurs will attempt to claw back from their disastrous first leg away to FC Sporting Saliva of Bucharest. Manager Hussey is confident of reversing that tragedy now that striker Alan Yentob has been pronounced fit by the team dentist: "Alan had bloody abysmal luck in Romania,

he bent his upper plate on a gritty hamburger before we'd even left Heathrow and then went and broke his lower one trying to open a bottle of Newcastle Brown on the plane. He just couldn't put them together on the night."

'After the football, there's *Pot Anything You Can Manage* from Ilford Women's Snooker Institute, which pits Mrs Hurricane Emsworth, who is colour-blind, against Mother Elvira, a drunk. The coveted *Sportsnight* trophy will go to the player incurring the fewest holes in the cloth.

'At 4.45, it's time for *Not Quite Celebrity Pro-Am Yo-Yo*, when the Elvis Presley Nearly Lookalike XV takes on the Could Almost Be Elton John in a Bad Light Team for a place in next Sunday's final, after which it's over to the Albert Hall (the Albert Hall who cleans Liz Forgan's windows) for his special presentation of *Late Night Boxing Line-Up*, a fascinating computer contest which will settle once and for all the old argument over who, if Wolfgang Amadeus Mozart had fought Rocky Marciano for the World Heavyweight String Quartet title, would have won. A nearly-new IBM 780, programmed with both men's musical and pugilistic records, will match them over 15 rounds, inter-round commentaries from Sarah Dunant talking to Frank Bruno's uncle, and song of praise for the winner from Thora Hird, accompanied on the ringside bell by Michael Fish.'

Something for all sports fans there, eh?

Child's Play

I was delighted to read last Monday's reports that Gyles Brandreth MP was to make a film explaining the workings of the EC to his fellow Tories, since it strongly suggested that the complaints concerning this Government's lack of intellectual gravitas and political depth had not, as many of us had feared, gone unheeded by Conservative Central Office.

That this was indeed the case was proved within seconds of my telephoning Sir Norman Fowler for corroboration, when I learned that Mr Brandreth's great visionary work will not stand alone but be merely the first of many similar major policy studies.

Scripts have now been commissioned for *Thomas the Tank Engine Gets Privatized*, *Charley and the Rover Factory*, *Rebecca of Sunnybrook Subsidy*, *Alice in Receivership*, *What Katy Did for British Aerospace*, and *Winnie-the-Pooh Finally Gets His Hernia Seen To*, while shooting has already started on *William Looks for Work*, *Five Go Off to Hong Kong* and *Millie-Mollie-Mandy Shuts a Mine*.

In short, except for the slight hiccup involved in remaking *Noddy Joins the ERM* as *Noddy Quits the ERM*, things in Toytown have never looked better.

Gardening Notes: No 187

Now that all climbers, ramblers and border plants have shed their leaves and been pruned back so that you can see what's what, it is the ideal time to get together with your neighbour over the question of repairs to communal fences and trellises that have deteriorated or even collapsed under the weight of summer growth. I have always found that the best implement for dealing with this tricky problem is a small hammer. If you have a big neighbour, then use a big hammer.

'Ello 'Ello, What's All This Then?

I wonder if I am alone in being somewhat uneasy at the introduction by the Lancashire Constabulary, thanks to a recessionary shortage of real vehicles, of glass fibre Range Rover cut-outs, with a similarly two-dimensional cardboard copper at the wheel, which have been propped up along the hard shoulder of the M55 to deter speeding motorists. Might they not prove to be, quite literally, the thin end of the wedge?

True, the experiment seems, so far, to have succeeded in reducing speed. Possibly out of curiosity, since many motorists will have been intrigued by the sight of a police vehicle waving gently in the breeze and slowed for a more informative shufti, but even though it can surely be only a matter of time before hysterically cackling drivers start swerving into one another, that is not what most worries me. Now that word

of these curious items is out, and snaps of them have appeared in the national Press, how long can it be before our enterprising hooligans decide to descend upon them and knock them about for a giggle?

Should this threaten, the demonstrably hard-pressed Lancashire Constabulary will, I suppose, be forced to introduce two-dimensional beat officers, perhaps with cardboard alsatians, to be dotted about on motorway banks to deter vandals from charging down them and attacking their cardboard colleagues. It will not of course do so, particularly after a few real alsatians have had a go at the dummies (possibly in quite unsavoury ways), or even the odd peckish hedgehog.

Where the old Lancashire Bill goes from there is anybody's guess. Inflatable police helicopters attached to long strings must be on the cards, or even large Assistant

Commissioners in rolled-up trousers and green baize aprons offering one another cardboard masonic hand-shakes, but what will any of this achieve but further provocation to which enterprising villains will unquestionably rise in retaliation?

And that is my real fear. Any day now, glass fibre burglars will begin appearing on Lancastrian drainpipes, plywood muggers will be lurking in dark alleyways, and hardly a bank, building society, or sub-post office will fail to have a few dodgy dummies loitering nearby with obvious intent.

The police will be run ragged. They will not know what has hit them. They will be beyond all coping. I give the brains behind all this, Chief Superintendent Geoff Meadows, fair warning: you have sown the wind, and you will reap the whirlwind. You are about to be blown flat.

Give Them the Tools and We Will Finish the Job

I was greatly relieved to read Alan Clark's stirring justification of British arms sales to Iraq on the grounds that it was a jolly good idea to supply an enemy with weapons whose exact capability you would know if the enemy then turned round and pointed them at you.

Relieved, because it means that the truth can at last be told which will allow the much maligned Neville Chamberlain to reap the glory of which he has been cheated for more than half a century. Ever since, in fact, that fateful thirties day on which the brilliant Surbiton machine-tool manufacturer Arthur Junkers took him up for a spin in his new Stuka, in the hope that the Prime Minister would buy it for the RAF.

Chamberlain, however, had a far better plan: much

Right Hassim, step one, glue part A to part B.

impressed with this remarkable dive-bombing tool, he suggested that Arthur let him sell it to Germany, so that we in Britain would know precisely what was hitting us, if it ever did. Older readers, indeed, may remember Chamberlain returning waving Hitler's cheque, though, of course,

the canny old bird never let on that that was what it was.

This brilliant export stratagem enabled Adolf to launch his blitzkrieg against Poland, without which the Second World War might never have started, and we should thus have been prevented, six years later, from winning it.

Postscript

Today is Petula Clark's 59th birthday, and the Post Office joins me in reminding her that tomorrow is the last day for sending the following Christmas mail:

Bugle mutes to Sarawak; fancy rats (caged) and omnibus parts to Minorca; models of Trevor Macdonald to North (but not South) Uzeira; anything with a hole in it to New Guinea; garden furniture (excluding sideboards) to Liberia; inlaid floors, books about saucepans, and ringworm ointment to Peru; men's table-lamps to Estonia.

A Bogus Patient Writes

Dear Sir,

I do not know which way to turn. I have just learned that the doctor I have been registered with for the past 10 years is bogus. This was brought to my attention by a letter he sent saying he had been transferred to a large group practice at Parkhurst, where he is registered as Dr 17789954 and may be consulted between 2 pm and 3 on alternate Thursdays, but please do not bang on the glass. Also, he will no longer require me to strip off when calling for a repeat prescription.

The fact is, it may be all my fault. It is extremely boring in Hayes, and in 1982, for want of anything better to do, I went into his surgery and told him I thought my liver had fallen off in the night. He was very sympathetic and said it was a common condition, livers were held on only by three little screws which could easily come undone after sex. He gave me two Smarties, and told me to come back in an hour to see if they'd worked, we could test them out on his couch. We did this and he said my liver was now firmly in place, the Smarties had done the trick.

Over the next 10 years he treated me for all sorts of things I thought up, a broken ear, distemper, lime-scale, a whistling foot, greenfly, you name it. He was a wonderful doctor: once, when I told him I thought my lungs were growing, he just said not to worry, there was a lot of it about, it was due to having a big bust, so I asked him if I could have a second opinion and he said, yes, you have nice legs as well.

Then, a few weeks ago, the police came round and asked if it was true I was being given regular treatment for a faulty carburettor at a hotel in Uxbridge, and the next thing I knew they had taken him away.

I am at my wit's end. Do you have the address of a bogus psychiatrist?

Yours etc

Lava-bred

I was astonished at the outrage expressed by Italian environmentalists over tomorrow's opening of a McDonald's restaurant at Pompeii to cater for the four million tourists who annually visit the ruins.

These whingeing numskulls clearly have no knowledge whatever of their own history. For it was at this very spot, 1,913 years ago, that not only the hamburger itself was born but also the entire wonderful concept of fast-food takeaway.

In AD 79 Pompeiians who had fled Vesuvius's initial eruption returned to their flattened homes to find that the lava had also rolled over their farm animals. Hacking away the pumice, they discovered, beneath it, that their cows were now ten metres wide and a centimetre thick, ground to a pulp and done to a turn. Furthermore, their chickens had been reduced to sizzling nuggets. With nothing else to eat in their devastated homes, they immediately fell upon these char-broiled remains and, to their astonished delight, found them remarkably tasty.

It was at this point that the volcano's second eruption began, leaving the panic-stricken townsfolk no option, as the torrents of molten rock rolled once more towards them, but to snatch up the food, as fast as possible, and take it away with them.

The Latin for mincemeat is *amberga*.

Oh Come Ye of Fairly Little Faith . . .

Following the proposal of the former Bishop of London that Synod-disaffected Anglicans should up sticks and join the Catholic church, thousands of you have naturally written to me for my expert advice.

'All right,' you say, 'we do not want to go to church of a Sunday and have a woman tell us how to lead our lives, we get enough of that all week, thank you very much, never mind 13 years of Margaret bloody Wossname, but we do not want to become Roman Catholics, either, all that confession stuff, you never know who's listening, plus incense on your best suit and never certain where you are when it comes to how's your father, or should I say how's your Father, ha-ha-ha, so are

there any other religions you can suggest which might suit me? I am not what you would call religious, but it's always useful to have something to put on the form when applying for a road fund licence, etcetera.'

A tricky one, this, since I do not have the space to go into great detail, but knowing the British as I do, I think I may at least come up with a few helpful pointers for those in what we theologians call doubt.

Judaism has considerable appeal. The soup is good, and you can keep your hat on indoors, thereby saving on fuel costs. Also, books are read back to front, which means you do not have to plough through the whole of the new Jeffrey Archer to find out what happens.

Islam may suit you even better, in that if you don't want to read the new Jeffrey Archer at all, you can not only burn it, you can apply to have him shot. The main drawback with Islam is that you take your shoes off on entering a mosque. If it is a big mosque, it may take you all day to find them again.

Buddhism is terrific if you are bald. No one will ever know. You can also spend all day walking up and down Oxford Street without having to buy anything. Furthermore, the principle of reincarnation is very attractive. You could come back as the Sultan of Brunei. But then again, you could come back as Jeffrey Archer.

Hinduism likewise has both pros and cons. You do

not have to find your own wife, which saves you a fortune in flowers, chocolates and perfume, but you have to stay open until midnight, all week, because you can never tell when a non-Hindu might want to buy flowers, chocolates and perfume. You may also have to stock the new Jeffrey Archer, if it looks like being a goer.

So there you are. Good luck. And remember, too, that the **Mormons** are always on the lookout for new recruits. They're a nice crowd, with only one drawback: you have to wear a blue suit and a permanent grin and tell everybody about this wonderful book of yours. You will thus run the constant risk of being mistaken for Jeffrey Archer.

A Church Mouse Writes

Dear Sir,

You will not need to be told I am poor, you are reading this off of a bit of brown paper bag, I cannot afford nothing white with lines on, let alone Basildon Bond, also you will have noticed that my letter is a bit nibbled under the signature due to where there was a smear of jam on the paper, and you do not turn your nose up at a nice smear of jam if you are as poor as a church mouse, the bag probably had a doughnut in it at some time, whatever

that is, I wouldn't know, I have never seen a doughnut, I am not an executive mouse, I am not a factory mouse, I am not even a bloody council house mouse, I am lucky to have two crumbs to rub together and a roof over my head, albeit one with the lead stripped off and the rain widdling in, God knows what happened to the appeal fund, that big red cardboard thermometer outside hasn't moved since a drunk put two bob in the slot in 1964, and

that was by mistake, he was after ten Weights.

And now look. Any minute now, I will not even have crumbs. I will not even have a roof with holes in. I will be out on my ear. Don't talk to me about the ordination of women, there's two things I know about women, and they are (a) the place has to be spotless, and (b) mice have to be dead. Show me a female vicar and I will show you (a) a floor you could eat your dinner off of, unless of course you

were a mouse, ie no crumbs or them nice green bits of old Spam, and (b) mousetraps. When it comes to women vicars it is 'Let us sing "All Creatures That On Earth Do Dwell Except Mice"', it is 'Blessed are the poor, unless they are church mice, in which case use a baseball bat', it is 'And the greatest of these is charity, provided it is not a mouse on the receiving end'.

I tell you, this is the end of Christianity as we know it.

Yours etc

Nice Little Earners

I rather fear that, by insisting that Her Majesty the Queen start paying income tax, the nation may well have opened a Pandora's can of worms which will end up costing us dear.

I have been in discussion with both the Inland Revenue and the Department of Health and Social Security, and, believe me, I know whereof I speak.

To begin with, in paying income tax, Her Majesty will automatically be making National Insurance contributions. These will render her eligible for benefit amounting to £41.20 per week. Thus, to take a recent example, in the event of her waking up on the morning of a major Guildhall speech and finding that she has a nasty cough and can hardly squeak, she will not have to turn up to deliver it. All she has to do is fill in Form SC1 and enclose a note from her doctor saying she is feeling a bit crook, and the money will come in anyway. She can then go back to bed with a tankard of Lemsip and the new Jilly Cooper, leaving several hundred people in

expensive new hats and best suits to turn up and wonder (a) who that woman is sitting between the Lord Mayor and Prince Philip, and (b) why they are all listening to a speech by Jimmy Tarbuck. If, furthermore, she is off work for more than six months, the sickness benefit will become invalidity benefit, hiking her weekly income up to a staggering £54.15. This money will of course be paid by you and me.

But it does not end there. Her new status also

makes her eligible for unemployment benefit, payable in the event of no suitable work being forthcoming. Let us assume that it happens to be something of a slack period in the royal calendar: there are no parliaments to open, no ships to be launched, no investitures to be held, no foreign heads of state turning up wanting a hot dinner, and all National Hunt meetings have been cancelled due to soggy going. Under these circumstances, Her Majesty

would be fully entitled to go down to her local Job Centre, inquire if there were any openings for a trained queen, and, upon being told that there was nothing on the books at present, collect £43.10.

So let us not leap to congratulate ourselves on manoeuvring our gracious sovereign into a corner from which there was no escape. The boot was on the other foot all the time. She is a clever woman. There are no flies on her. She saw us coming.

Gardening Notes: No 413

Now is the time of year to start thinking about sowing next year's vegetable crop, because no other area of the garden requires quite as much preparation, if disappointment is to be avoided.

First, you will need to buy a new Renault. You can of course, under EC legislation, make do with a new Citroen or Peugeot, but the French Government is particularly keen to encourage investment in Renault at this time, and when you write to the French Consulate General (21 Cromwell Road, SW7) for permission to grow vegetables in your garden, it will help your cause considerably if you enclose a photostat of a Renault logbook. Should, however, you have at least one French grandparent, you may get away with proof of owning only a French bicycle, provided, of course, that you have never used it to sell onions.

Once your application has been received, the Consul will send an official team to inspect your garden, so do be sure you have a French greenhouse (flying a tricolour on it, though not strictly demanded under the CAP, would be a smart move), a set of French garden tools, two big balls of French twine, a 20-kilo bag of Jean Innes Numéro 2 potting compound, and (but only if you can prove it comes from a French stable) a large heap of fresh merde. You are now ready, if your French is good enough to fill in the 18-page questionnaire, to apply for your annual honorary French farmership (1,000 francs; children under 12 half-price, if their plot does not exceed 2 square metres). Once this is granted, you will be permitted to commence planting, provided, naturally, that the Elysée Palace's quote is rigorously adhered to: if, for example, yours is an average suburban garden, you will be allowed 6 lettuces, 4 bunches of radishes, 2 cauliflowers, 9 beetroot, 14 carrots and 138 pea-pods (but no mange-tout). Be warned, however, that your permission jardinière may be revoked at any time should you fail your monthly inspection or be caught drinking anything but bordeaux, burgundy or champagne, and also that the permit itself does not represent a guarantee against unofficial action by visiting French farmers. Indeed, despite Berkshire Fire Department's investigation, the strongest suspicions remain that Her Majesty's Windsor gardeners may have been caught growing French beans without a licence.

A Celebrity Square Writes

Dear Sir,

Gorblimey is that the *time?*

Yes, it's me, I need no introduction, I cannot walk down the street without people shouting *Gorblimey is that the time?*, it is probably the most famous catchphrase in the history of the world, I do not know how they recognize me off the screen but they do, can it be my yellow tuxedo, can it be my diamante trainers, can it be my two-foot Havana, can it be the personalized number plate under my arm, no, I don't think so, I think it is because I give off this, I dunno, incredible warmth, this sheer bloody personality I have, it is not my fault people get trampled trying to pull signed photographs out of my minders' sacks, I did not ask to be universally loved, it was just summink I was born with.

It is also summink the BBC ought to think about bloody hard before making a very big mistake. Have you seen what they have proposed in last week's Green Paper? They have only proposed drastic reductions in game shows! I mean, gorblimey is that the time, or what? Do they realize what they are asking the people of this great country of ours to give up? Ever since I first achieved megastar status all them years ago as wacky gynaecologist Monty Dreck in the record-breaking West End drama *Whose Knickers Are These?* I have been the resident panellist in every major game show there has ever been, I have been the star of *Guess My Smell, The Winkle Factor, Count up to Seven, The Cardboard Shot, Deaf Date, I've Got a Pig, Boncebusters, Win a Nice Teapot;* you name it, I have shouted 'Gorblimey is that the time?' on it, I am a national institution, if the BBC gives me the bullet millions will tear up their licences, there will be riots all over.

Never mind how supermarkets are going to get opened. Never mind how Bosnian cats' homes etcetera are going to get by without me playing celebrity pro-am golf for them. Never mind people going into shops and not knowing what to buy due to my face not being on the packets no more.

The country will not stand for it. I am what family entertainment is all about. I do not know who this John Berk is, all I know is he has just put his name to his own death warrant.

Yours, gorblimey is that the time etc

Be a Brick, Ma'am!

What a strange johnny a train of thought is! To what remarkable and fascinating destinations it can lead!

When I read last Thursday that Lego, the Danish toy firm, had bought the ailing Windsor Safari Park and intended to spend £60 million transforming it into a Legoland entertainment complex, my first thought was: how extraordinary that the figure should be £60 million, because that is the *precise* amount which our great Heritage Secretary said was required to restore Windsor Castle!

If your own train is on a faster track than mine, you will know what my second thought was.

Is there any good reason, now that we have found someone in a position to chuck around wads of £60 million we ourselves haven't got, not to invite the Danes to buy Windsor Castle, too?

By rebuilding it with little red and blue and yellow bricks, they would be able, at a stroke, not only to incorporate it tastefully within this new entertainment complex of theirs, but also to end the row currently raging between those who want the castle restored exactly as it was and those who want to seize the opportunity for modernizing it.

For the immense advantage of

Lego is that it can be rebuilt in the twinkling of an eye, and thereby satisfy all demands and tastes: Windsor Castle could be Norman one week, Georgian the next, post-Modern the week after that, it could be a mosque on Fridays, an Asda hypermarket on Saturdays, and a mock-Tudor dolphinarium on those Sundays when it wasn't being a neo-Classical funfair. Furthermore, since Lego already markets a range of Legopeople kits to enable you to populate your Lego houses, trains, cars, and so forth, we could be well on the way here to solving all the besetting problems of the Monarchy.

After all, it is generally agreed that the Royal Family are primarily figureheads, so I fail to see why the present incumbents should not be quietly retired and replaced with a Royal Legofamily. They could ride about in state coaches, assemble in a waving position on balconies, stand around in paddocks, sail the world in *Britannia*, and if the tabloids, or popular opinion, or whatever, suddenly took against this one or that, he or she could instantly be remodelled or replaced, at a fraction of the present fuss and cost.

I think the Heritage Secretary should look into it.

An Envelope Writes

Dear Sir,

I think I speak for all envelopes when I say that this is the happiest day of my life!

I do not know if you have ever considered what the lot of the average member of my profession is like, it is a nightmare from start to finish.

You lie there 50 to a packet like bloody sardines until it is time for some ratbag to lick your back, you never know where that tongue has been, then you get banged flat, have another licked thing stuck on your front, and after that it's through the slot to lie in the dark for God knows how long with five hundred other miserable sods all whingeing on about flap-abuse until it's time to get bunged into some foul-smelling sack and driven up the sorting-office for throwing about. And the next thing you know, if all goes according to plan, their plan, not yours, some swine is poking a knife or, worse, finger, through you prior to screwing you up and bunging you in the fire or bin.

Not what you would call a distinguished career, is it? The only thing in its favour is the opportunities for travel. I am not of course referring here to those of us unlucky enough to get where it says on our fronts, some poor blighters set off from N14 and never get further than N16 before ending up on the scrap-heap, I am referring to all those of us who, due to this Royal Mail cock-up and that, may well find theirselves being redirected half a dozen times, very exciting, you never know where you're going. Could be Warrington, could be Isleworth, could be both and next week Galashiels, I heard of a co-worker who got posted early for Christmas 1978, bound for West Drayton, and did not arrive until Easter 1991, he had seen Johannesburg, Wembley, St Petersburg, you name it. He went to his bin happy, I can tell you.

That is why this is such a great day for me.

I have just learned that the Post Office is shedding 16,000 staff, mainly in sorting-offices; this will change the face of travel as we know it, very soon now the vast majority of us will be hurtling about like nobody's business, I have always fancied seeing Tahiti, myself, possibly stopping off in New York and Glasgow, maybe a fortnight in Antibes, you never know your luck.

You will have noticed that this letter has come to you by fax. I did not want to bring it myself, due to where I might have got to you next day, and I am, as I say, hoping for better things in the near future.

I mean, we are constantly being told we only pass this way but once, am I right, but if there's a chance we could pass it 47 times, I think we should go for it.

Yours etc

How Was It For You?

Partly because I had nothing better to do, but mainly because the *Sunday Express* gave me a million pounds to do it, I have spent the past few days conducting a survey of 18,876 men and women who have read the Wellcome Report on British sexual behaviour, so that my findings can be put on a shelf somewhere for the benefit of sociologists who may one day wish to use them to conduct a survey into the best ways of getting organizations to cough up a million pounds. Of those buttonholed, 32 per cent said that the survey was terrific for them, they had enjoyed every minute of it, they were totally satisfied and they could not wait to read it again, 39 per cent said that it was all right, but not as good as they had expected, they did not know what all the fuss was about, 20 per cent said they would just as soon have had a hot dinner, and nine per cent said they had been absolutely disgusted, they felt, oh, sort of dirty, they would never go near sociology again. Not surprisingly, the 16–30 age group read it most quickly, 1.3 minutes on average, the 31–49 band took 7.9 minutes, those in the 50–69 bracket spent between 14.3 and 32.8 minutes, and a 93-year-old Cricklewood man who started reading it last Wednesday was, when I telephoned him last night, still struggling to get past page four. On the wider demographic stage, I discovered that while the majority had read it in bed at night (more or less evenly divided between those who had read it before their cocoa and those who had read it after), 18 per cent had read it in the bath, nine per cent on the kitchen table, and six per cent in a number of quite remarkable locations, including one man who claimed to have read it three times in a Boeing 747 at 40,000 feet. One interesting minor statistic is that all the MPs questioned had read it during the afternoon, breaking off when the division bell rang and, after they had voted, returning to their nearby hotel to finish it

A Royal Toast-rack Writes

Dear Sir,

Since leaving Harrod's in 1981, I have been employed as Toast-rack-in-Waiting to Their Royal Highnesses the Prince and Princess of Wales. As is so often the way with public office, mine is boring, uncomfortable, and sometimes hazardous work: it is bad enough standing around all morning with flunkeys poking hot Wonderloaf in you every five minutes, without being chucked at the wall on a regular basis due to this tantrum or that. I have copped so many dents it has become impossible to decipher my hall-mark, I could be bloody EPNS for all you can tell, and on one occasion my knob broke off entirely after sudden contact with someone's head, no names, no pack drill, and had to be put back with superglue, due to which it is now permanently wonky.

But I do not complain. That is what public service is all about. That is what duty means. You will not catch me banging on and on to, say, the jam-dish, about how wretched my life is, what a mistake I have made, Jammy, what is to become of me etcetera and so forth, any more than you would catch the jam-dish running away with the spoon. We have made our bed and we have got to lie in it, life is a matter of swings and wossnames, ours not to reason why, follow my drift?

What compensates for it is one's status. That is one's reward. Which brings one to one's point: in all the current rabbiting about who now does what where and all the rest of it, nobody has said anything at all about the constitutional position of toast-racks. I could not believe it. I have all the papers lying next to me of a morning, and there has not been one single bloody word in any of them about what the future holds for royal silverware. I could well end up not being royal at all: when they come to divvy up the marital gear, I could find myself going to her premises, and what then, next thing you know there's a divorce, she re-marries, and I am looking at life as a truckdriver's toast-rack, they do not even use them, they just grab it straight from the toaster, he'll probably have me down the shed holding seed-packets, and if he's short of a few bob come Walthamstow dog-night I might well have to face the humiliation of a pawnbroker pointing out my wonky knob.

Mind you, would it be any better if the Prince got me? Most of the cutlery here — and they know whereof they speak, they have seen them all come and go — reckon he will never be king. The smart money is on him going off to live in a cave, he will not have formal breakfast in a cave, anyway he'll probably want to live off roots and berries etcetera, being him.

I just want to know where I stand. The Prime Minister should make a statement in the House. This is the worst crisis in our history since Wallis Simpson walked off with a full set of Queen Mary's saucepans.

Yours etc

We are Fred Patten's Army

On Monday, a MORI poll revealed that Britain's 7-year-olds did not know when William the Conqueror invaded, when the Spanish Armada sailed, when World War Two ended, what the Greenhouse Effect was, or where Bosnia, New Zealand, Canada or even Great Britain were. The only fact they all knew was that they could start buying booze at 18.

I sympathize completely. If 12 years of education have left you with nothing but the belief that you are living somewhere which could well be not only part of Yugoslavia but also overrun by Frenchmen pouring across the border from New Zealand, besieged by an enormous Spanish Fleet lying off Canada a mere five miles away, and likely to be bombed by the Luftwaffe with deadly greenhouse gases any moment now, it is hardly surprising that you should be counting the days until you can get your hands on a bottle of something to take your mind off it.

A Brief History of Christmas

274 The Emperor Aurelian chooses 25 December as the birthday of the unconquered sun (*natalis solis invicti*). To celebrate the event, his wife buys him a pair of gloves (*tegumenta digitalia*). They do not fit (*inutilis*).

336 With the arrival of Christianity in Rome, the Church establishes the birthday of Christ on the same date. To celebrate the event, the Emperor Constantine asks his wife for a set of ring-spanners. He gets gloves.

541 Resistance to the concept of Christmas by Jerusalem is finally overcome, and it is celebrated there for the first time. Most scholars now accept that the reason for the delay was that it took two centuries for the idea of gloves to spread eastwards.

583 The first appearance of holly as a Christmas decoration. This was adopted from a pagan regeneration rite which marked that time of year when things began to look up for greengrocers.

709 Christmas arrives in England, prompting the Venerable Bede to write his first book. He thereafter writes one a year to catch the Christmas market, culminating in 731 with his biggest-seller, *Historia Ecclesiastica Gentis Anglorum*, translated into the vernacular as *The Country Diary of an Anglo-Saxon Gentleman*. He dies in Jarrow, but his remains are moved to Durham on Christmas Day 1031, to coincide with the re-issue of the paperback.

881 Hiding from the Danes in Athelney, King Alfred is forced to spend Christmas alone. Realizing this means another year without new gloves, he begins to drink heavily, spilling brandy on to his cake. Ignited by a spark, this then burns down; but since he has nothing else to eat, he rapidly devours the remains, with post-Christmas consequences which doctors have been recognizing for 1,100 years.

929 Death of Wenceslas, King of Bohemia. Cause of death never cleared up: was he attacked by an old man collecting faggots, or an old faggot collecting men? (cf. 'Heat was in the very sod . . .')

1066 With the Norman victory at Hastings on 16 October, a peculiar French practice is introduced whereby every year, on 16 October to commemorate the conquest, bands of mercenaries wander the streets, banging on doors and singing unintelligible (possibly Old French) songs, and demanding money with menaces. They go on doing this every night until Christmas.

Carol singers! Fetch the mince pies and boiling oil!

1191 Sensing the vast marketing possibilities of laying copyright claims to Nazareth, the Third Crusade embarks for the Holy Land with a view to securing the Christmas card franchise. The Turks and Syrians fiercely resist this, since they control the fig, date, and mincemeat trade, and fear it will be undermined if housewives prefer to spend their Christmas Club payouts on rhyming correspondence.

1192 Returning to England, King Richard's men discover their wives being kissed in the hall by strange men. The wives explain that this is a new magical method of removing mistletoe from joists.

1193 Richard and his army embark for France. The fighting continues for some years. Returning to England, his men discover that they have several new children. Their wives explain that, every Christmas, a man climbs down the chimney.

1194 At Santa's Sherwood Grotto, the monumentally nasty Sheriff of Nottingham disguises himself as Father Christmas so that he can disappoint as many children as possible. Little Robin of Locksley is asked what he wants, and says gloves. He is given a bow and arrow.

1215 At Runnymede, the barons present their demands to King John. Each baron asks for a Meccanoe sette, a footballe, a jacke-knyfe with eight thynges onne it, a Ninja Turtle bresteplate, and a dogge.

1348 During Christmas dinner preparations for Edward III, a goose is put in too hot an oven by the royal chef, and explodes. Fearing the king's wrath, the cook scrapes the skin off the ceiling, sews it together, and frantically stuffs it with anything he can sweep off the floor. Despite the fact that the Black Death subsequently devastates England, the recipe remains traditional to this day.

1476 Caxton sets up his press at Westminster. His first commission comes from the Duke of Gloucester (later Richard III) who asks Caxton to set: 'Merrie Xmas and I donte thynke, har, har, har!' The message is then put in a twist of festive paper containing a small bomb and sent by Richard to his brother, Edward IV. However, the gift is intercepted by two footmen, each of whom claims to have seen it first; in the ensuing tug-of-war, the paper tube rips apart and the bomb explodes, killing both men.

1478 The first printed party invitation. It is Caxton's second commission from the Duke of Gloucester (later Richard III), and reads 'Merrie Xmas, we are havynge a few people over for drynkes, nothynge formal, do droppe in, har, har, har!' This is sent round to the Duke of Clarence, attached to a butt of malmsey.

1483 Introduction of the scarf as a popular Christmas gift. Richard III (formerly the Duke of Gloucester)

sends two round to the Tower for his nephews, personally delivered by the Court Strangler; who is also, incidentally, the first man to have remarked, 'I wouldn't bother with Christmas, if it wasn't for the kids.'

1588 Armada sunk. British sherry introduced.

1589 273 separate salvage attempts on Spanish wrecks.

1590 Potatoes and cigars introduced to Elizabeth's court at Christmas dinner by Sir Walter Raleigh. They are not a success: the Queen is unable to light her croquette, and the Earl of Essex surreptitiously gives his boiled panatellas to the cat.

1603 Accession of James VI of Scotland as James I of England, heralding the introduction of tartan slippers.

1662 Several Plymouth pilgrims arrive back from the New World, bringing turkeys, to spend Christmas with their relatives. First hot roast turkey eaten.

1663 Last cold roast turkey eaten.

1664 Last turkey risotto polished off.

1665 Great Plague.

1689 William of Orange accedes to English throne, introducing many interesting Dutch fashions. At Christmas, 847 people die of advokaat.

1733 John Kay invents the flying shuttle, revolutionizing the textile industry. At Christmas, loved ones excitedly exchange three million dressing-gowns with one another. After Christmas, they are exchanged again, this time for credit notes. John Kay put in stocks by shopkeepers and pelted with unsold gloves, tartan slippers and bottles of advokaat.

1785 Edmund Cartwright invents the power loom. First mass-produced beige cardigans begin appearing in dustbins.

1825 The first railway, from Stockton to Darlington,

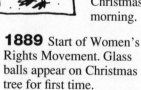

is opened. Next day, it is broken. The Minister of Transport gets a clout from his father.

1849 Prince Albert introduces the Christmas tree to England, filling Balmoral with needles. In retaliation, Queen Victoria gets a bagpiper to play under their bedroom window every Christmas morning.

1889 Start of Women's Rights Movement. Glass balls appear on Christmas tree for first time.

1901 The Berlin family, recently arrived in America from Russia, is so poor it has to live in Harlem, where Irving is four feet too short to play basketball with the neighbourhood kids. On Christmas Eve, he is staring miserably out of the window, sighing, when his father asks

him what he is dreaming of. Pretty soon, the family is so rich it can move to Long Island, where Irving learns golf.

1914 Christmas Day soccer fixture between England and Germany, on neutral Flanders ground, ends in unprecedented scenes of crowd violence. Rival supporters fight it out for four years. Germany subsequently demands replay.

1923 John Logie Baird spends ghastly Christmas watching his children screaming over busted chemistry sets, listening to his wife's Uncle Norman reciting *The Green Eye of the Little Yellow God*, forcing a tyre-lever between his brother-in-law and the parlourmaid, trying to remove advokaat from the piano hammers, and staring at 18 pairs of new gloves which do not fit him. Baird decides that there has to be a better way of passing the festive season than this. Time, however, proves that he could not have been more wrong.

Animal Crackers

Since thousands of you have written in begging for suggestions as to what to buy your pets this Christmas, the *Sunday Express* has set up an exclusive Xmaspetmart™ to help solve those tricky gift problems. All items are available at *Sunday Express* shops everywhere.

'Qui Est un Joli Garçon, Alors?'

Yes, it's true! At last, your budgie can learn the French they speak in France! This tiny peckproof cassette-player, which begins to play as soon as its owner runs up the attached ladder, comes complete with four weeny records: *At the Customs*, *At the Chemist*, *At the Beach*, and *In the Hospital*. Not only will this enable your bird to form many new friendships here and abroad, it will also make him an invaluable helpmeet on your travels together. Only £7.95, excl. batt. *Also available*: Spanish, Welsh, Romanian, Urdu, and (for larger birds only) Pidgin.

Rubber Burglar! A Steal at £9.95!

At last, something for Rover really to get his teeth into! For years now, man's best friend has been stuck each Yuletide with the outdated rubber bone when only 2.7 per cent of Britain's dogs know what a bone is, in these days of tinned marrowbone-enriched soya. Yet a staggering 88.9 per cent in these criminal times know what a burglar is! Nor is our rubber burglar any old length of inanimate sorbo: bite it, and it flails its arms about realistically, lets out a blood-curdling shriek, and wets its trousers. *Also available*: rubber bailiff, rubber VAT inspector, and rubber brother-in-law.

The Hwang Lu Fok Miniature Submarine Gymnasium

How often the proud owner of a Siamese fighting fish, showing off his pet to a guest, finds himself facing the embarrassing question: 'Yes, very nice, but who's he beaten recently?' Because the truth is that generations of domestication have reduced the species to nothing more than a flabby shadow of its magnificent primitive self.

Now, this miniature fitness centre will change all that! *Contains*: tiny punchball, bicycle, weights, tracksuit, gloves, jockstrap, plus list of nearest 12 opponents to your home. Only £29.95.

Gifts for the Smaller Pet

- **Dayglo Fun T-Shirts for Worms**.
Easy to fit, no messy gluing, just £1.95 each. If ordering by mail, please specify Earth, Slow, or Tape.
- **Is Your Stick Insect Lonely?**
Banish those solitude blues with a *Sunday Express* Bunch of Twigs, 25p, includes several erotic shapes.
- **Prawn Cocktail**.
Dry martini, whisky sour, gin sling or pina colada, complete in individual thimble containing tiny straw, umbrella, and swizzle-stick, with half-peanut on the side, £1.95 each (napkins not included).
- **Have You Got Fleas?**
Why not buy them a hedgehog this Christmas? Provides hours of nourishing fun for a mere £5.95. Or flat, ex-M40, one driver only, £2.95.

Grand Christmas Quiz Answers

Because many of you, I know, prefer quizzes to probing questionnaires, last week I set 10 questions to enable readers to have a bit of good wholesome family fun around the festive board. Due, however, to a series of unforeseen bottle incidents during Christmas, the questions fell out of my teeth while I was attempting to crawl to the *Sunday Express* offices, and something else got printed instead. This week, due to a series of unforeseen bottle incidents during New Year's Eve, I found myself unable to focus on what to write in this space, so I have therefore decided to print the answers to last week's questions.

1. 1–0, after extra time. The penalty was taken by Queen Victoria.

2. A canteen of cutlery. The camel was found in a Cheltenham hotel.

3. *'Ich bin ein Frankfurter.'* He was thrown into the Rhine.

4. A kind of whisky, made from conkers.

5. Norman Lamont is the odd one out. All the rest are badgers.

6. An ear. She was sent to prison for six months.

7. Marlene Dietrich, because George Formby's was smaller.

8. 138 eggs and a herringbone overcoat. He died in Brussels.

9. The so-called Cardboard Bastard Case. Both bishops were defrocked.

10. Selena Scott. The ointment was immediately withdrawn from sale.

Sam Missiles Latest

While I can only applaud — and I know I speak for all of you — the sterling efforts of Miss Samantha Fox to get herself flown into the remains of Yugoslavia to do her bit for the British Army, I nevertheless fear for the incalculable repercussions should her bid prove successful.

I am led to this conclusion following long telephone conversations not only with Lord Owen and Cyrus Vance, but also with large numbers of senior spokespersons from all sides of the conflict, whose for once unanimous view was that the deployment of Miss Fox would represent an escalation likely to trigger a response which the UN would be powerless to control. Serbia, for example, made it abundantly clear that the boost for British troops would create so exponential an advance in morale-technology that it would have no other course than to deploy Kylie Josipovicenovic, whose 38–24–36 configuration and ability to mime to *One Of the Ruins That Serbia Knocked About a Bit* while dancing with an anaconda would bring their troops to a pitch of kamikaze hysteria.

Should that happen, Bosnia would almost certainly retaliate with the Sarajevo Girl Pipers, a 24-strong troupe of topless flautists whose recent tour of Bangkok was sadly cut short by excommunication, while informed sources are convinced that Saddam Hussein would not stand idly by but use this opportunity to gain a Balkan foothold by coming to the aid of dispirited Moslem forces with airborne belly-dancers flown from Baghdad and dropped en masse.

Were that to happen, the wider conflict could well force America's interventionist hand; though, when I spoke to them yesterday morning, Pentagon chiefs were not prepared to say whether, so early in his presidency, Bill Clinton would risk playing the Madonna card.

Mind How You Go

The new MoT test is apparently causing consternation to thousands of drivers failed for such infringements as chipped windscreens, scratched number plates, wonky wing-mirrors, rattling seatbelt-mounts, and all manner of previously permissible minutiae. In its defence, the Ministry has pointed out that while its object remains roadworthiness, it sees its wider remit as ensuring that driver's attention is not distracted by minor faults in his vehicle.

If you think this bodes yet worse, you are not wrong. I have before me a leaked document setting out the next test revisions, and unsettling reading it is. 'From 1/1/1994,' I note, 'little alsatians sitting on rear shelves will have to be able to nod both ways. If the head sticks at any point, or if one of the eyes has fallen out, the vehicle will be failed. It will also be failed if anything can be heard rolling about in the glove compartment, eg boiled sweet, dog's glass eye, etc, or if the ash-tray contains, for example, an old Elastoplast which could be ignited by an ineptly stubbed cigarette, thereby causing a fire leading to a multiple pile-up.

'While certain un-avoidable smells will be permitted — baby, garlic, old male relative, and so forth — odours such as cat, Guinness, or Chanel Number 5, indicating that things have been carried which could have distracted the driver's attention, may well lead to a criminal conviction.

'Also, stickers on bumpers and rear windows must not be in any way torn or defaced: signs, for instance, saying 'do it with their socks on,' or 'We have seen Lake,' will automatically fail a vehicle on the grounds that following drivers could be distracted by wondering who it is who do it with their socks on, or which lake might have been seen. In addition, little St Christopher statuettes will henceforth have to be screwed, not glued, to dashboards, since in the event of an emergency stop, these could fly off and lodge between the driver's legs, with well-nigh unfathomable consequences.

'A vehicle will also be refused a certificate if it has a wasp buzzing about in it, a spouse hitting the driver over the head with a road-map, or a child who should have gone before he left the house.'

A Publisher Writes

Dear Sir,

It will not have escaped your notice that *Churchill: the End of Glory* is belting up the best-seller lists, and why not, there is nothing the Great British Public likes more than a so-called national hero getting a right seeing-to, but since your millions of readers may not be aware that John Charmley's biography is just one of many such, I crave the indulgence of your esteemed columns to notify them of some of my own forthcoming titles, due to where it is my bounden public duty not to chuck money around on advertisements, it does not grow on trees.

Here at Bandwagon Books plc, we are particularly proud of Roger Pipsqueak's major new work, *Dam All*. Mr Pipsqueak, acclaimed author of *Wellington: Putting the Boot In*, first had his attention drawn to the notorious Guy Gibson scandal while watching *The Dam Busters*. His trained historian's eye immediately spotted that the dams ostensibly being blown up were in fact cardboard models. From there, it was but a short step to proving that what Gibson actually attacked were themselves cardboard, and, moreover, that he never left Britain to do it, preferring to fly the

entire sortie from the comfort and safety of his Link trainer, with the wicked connivance of Barnes Wallis, inventor of the cardboard bomb, acting on instructions from the appalling Churchill, who desperately needed a major victory if he was not to find himself standing in Downing Street with a suitcase. The book is lavishly illustrated with totally conclusive drawings.

We are also utterly delighted with *A Right Pair of Poofters*, the true story of Mallory and Irvine, who ran away together up Mount Everest in 1924. In this controversial new study, representing days of research, Geoff Who, a leading Assistant Lecturer at the Barnoldswick Institute for Heating & Ventilation, delved into laundry bills and phone messages to prove beyond doubt that not only was Mallory a former lover of Douglas Haig, but Irvine was terrified of standing on anything higher than a brick. The book contains 12 pages of formerly unpublished snapshots of people in balaclavas who could very well be either of them.

And finally, *Goodbye Sailor!*, Captain Eric Birdseye's penetrating study of the first man not to sail round the world single-handed. Capt Birdseye, who has twice crossed the mighty Serpentine in his craft, *Number 43*, at last reveals the major BBC gaffe which announced to an amazed world that Francis Chichester had circumnavigated the globe, whereas what in fact had happened was that Francis Globe had circumnavigated Chichester. The text has been corroborated by Syd Trevor-Roper.

I trust your readers will relish these major historical works. After all, wasn't it Henry Ford who said 'History is debunk'? No, it wasn't. It was said by Jane Austen, Desmond Morris, Cardinal Wolseley, and Old Mother Riley, all of whom manufactured small popular cars many years before Ford was even heard of.

Yours etc

Royal Hunt of the Sun

Old-fashioned I may be, but can I really be alone in deploring the brutal and calculated attempt by a few cynical megalomaniacs, with no consideration but their own gain, to undermine a unique, cherished, and time-honoured British institution?

For it is now abundantly clear that their frenzied battle to monopolize the tabloid market has led a handful of utterly unprincipled royals to threaten with destruction all that Fleet Street means.

Locked in their private circulation war, each determined to wipe the other out and thus dominate the news-stands, Charles and Diana have resorted to every dirty trick in the book, harassing reporters, suborning editors, embarrassing proprietors, bribing contacts, leaking secret documents, issuing unsubstantiated rumours through undisclosed sources, setting up bogus photo-opportunities . . . in short, unscrupulously deploying their power and their money to manipulate the public and distort the truth.

This reckless subversion of an ancient institution so dear to British hearts must cease forthwith! Fleet Street has suffered enough: the Monarchy should now leave it alone to get on with its life.

Furthermore, royals must be taught that power without responsibility has been the prerogative of the harlot down the ages: much as I thoroughly abhor the idea of introducing statutory controls to curb royal freedom, when that freedom is so flagrantly abused for personal advantage, something, surely, must be done.

Completely Barking

Dog-lovers who last week applauded all those critics complaining that Cruft's was out of touch with reality will be overjoyed to hear that, this week, the Campaign for Real Dogs will give its own annual awards.

I see from its Press release that the coveted Golden Scooper is going to Squat of Kentish Town III. Mongrel Squat not only succeeded in rendering half of Primrose Hill unfit for human use, he also killed the Queen Elizabeth Rose Garden in Regent's Park, fused nine street lamps in Finchley Road, and was directly responsible for having the phone box at Swiss Cottage melted down for scrap.

The, quite literally, runaway winner of The Tin Cowboy, donated by the Amalgamated Union of Panelbeaters, is the lovable border collie, Deaf. Although Deaf has only three legs, one eye and no tail, he still managed to cause 26 major road accidents in 1992 at a total repair cost of £89,836, his *pièce de résistance* being a five-car pile-up involving a Ferrari Testarossa, a 1904 Rolls-Royce Silver Ghost, a milk float, an 18-ton juggernaut, a panda car and a lollipop man.

The AUP's Glass Fibre Collar for Best Single Shunt, however, was won by Teensy-Weensy Chubbly Poppikins of Fawsley, a chihuahua who sprang from his owner's cleavage on the A40 and bit her on the ear, causing her to drive her new Corniche into a gravel bin at a cost of £17,357.

The BUPA Mug for watchdog work above and beyond the call of duty went, of course, to Uncontrollable Bastard IV of Securihound. Last July, Bastard, a thoroughbred pit doberweiler, was guarding the premises of Sam's Nearly New Carphone Lock-up plc when he noticed a Salvation Army band playing in the road outside.

Though trained only to take the throat out of VAT inspectors, Bastard nevertheless managed to bite his way through a chain-link fence and savage the entire woodwind section before tragically getting the worst of a valiant assault on a 137 bus.

Best of Show? Hard to say: the jury may well go for Haughey, the Irish wolfhound awarded the Confederation of Petfood Industry's Crystal Trough for devouring tins amounting to 1.8 whales and half a ton of minced donkey, or even Oscar Bravo Foxtrot, plucky alsatian winner of the West Midland Constabulary Cup for not only shoving a kilo of heroin under the Bishop of Cannock's mitre but also keeping him pinned to his altar until he confessed, but my own money is on Khazitex Prince II, the golden labrador who triumphantly carried off The Guild of Advertisers' Medal.

Any dog prepared to sprint non-stop from Land's End to John O' Groats and back again, paying out a 900-mile roll of lavatory paper as he ran, has got to be taken very seriously.

A Fox Writes . . .

Dear Sir,

I am not often appalled, it takes a lot to appal anyone in my game, you would not credit the sickening things you see on the hunting field, you need a strong stomach if you are going to spend your working life stumbling across members of the aristocracy lying under a hedge and going at it like knives, they ride with mobile phones these days so's they can fix theirselves up on the trot, some mornings I look over my shoulder just to see who's after me and there's nobody there, they have all paired up and dived off into the undergrowth, I can't remember the last time I had a decent workout.

But I am appalled now. It has come to my attention that in the House of Lords, the Earl of Caithness gave

assurances that the Channel Tunnel would not cause rabies, due to where French foxes would be kept out by, and I quote, 'a perimeter fence, a secure boundary, an electrified system inside the tunnel, and baited traps'.

I trust you have taken this in. I trust all its appalling implications have not been lost on you. This has absolutely nothing to do

with keeping French foxes out, it has everything to do with keeping British foxes in. What French fox in his right mind would run 30 miles through a hole in the sea just so's a lot of madmen could set their dogs on him?

Put another way, what British fox in his right mind *wouldn't,* just so's he could get away from them? It is no coincidence the Government

chose the House of Lords to give their assurances in, it is only nobs who are after the assurances, they are the ones who want to preserve field sports, eg rumpty-tumpty, how's your father, a lot on the side, I wish I was your trousers . . . need I go on?

I tell you, when it comes to cunning, foxes aren't in the same class.

Yours etc

Splashing Out

I hate to brag, but I must say I did do rather well at the Sotheby's sale of Maxwellibilia. I managed to make successful bids for a rather nice perpetual motion machine, never raced or rallied; a delightful little philosopher's stone for turning base metal into gold; a remarkably detailed map showing how to get to King Solomon's Mines by the 29 bus; an enormous white stuffed animal with astonishing tusks; and a

lovely piece of bright green cheese dug up from the moon and brought back to Lichtenstein by the fairies.

You will say, blimey, that lot must have set you back a bob or two! Not a bit of it: as soon as I told them what I intended buying, a number of banks began fighting among themselves for the chance to lend me the money. Not a word about when I have to pay it back, either.

Scalpel, Forceps, Broomstick

Shaken by last week's revelation that a Lincolnshire witches' coven had boasted two doctors among its members, I rushed out and bought a number of leading medical journals. As this extract from one of them shows, my worst fears were confirmed . . .

Treatment of Spinal Subdural Haematoma with Ferret's Ear

Spinal subdural haematoma is one of the rarer causes of acute spinal compression, and is usually associated with a bleeding diathesis. Here, a recent case is described in which the patient's condition was treated with the left ear of a dead ferret, specifically prepared.

Case Report: A man aged 59 presented with severe pains in the limbs and abdomen. A lumbar puncture yielded bloodstained fluid with xanthochromic supernatant containing 800mg of protein and 20mg of sugar per ml. CSF pressure was 45mm of CSF. There was severe flaccid paraparesis.

We waited until the night of the full moon, and slaughtered a male ferret in rut by striking it with the femur of a defrocked sexton. We then removed its ears. The right ear was nailed to the door of Lincoln Cathedral as a precaution (see *Treatment of Calcinosis Circumscripta with Stewed Mole*, BMJ, 1992, pp 177–181), and the left ear was brought to the Orthopaedic Research Unit of St Swithin's Hospital in a teapot. It was then swung round three times. We chalked a pentagram on the floor of the operating theatre, removed a live duck's giblets by the light of a candle, and took off our trousers. The patient was then premedicated by the anaesthetist, who shook a beaker of dried worms over him, murmuring 'Fee, fi, fo, fum, but especially fee', and brought into the theatre on a trolley drawn by six black cats. He was painted blue, and the left ear of the ferret was then pushed up his right nostril at the exact stroke of midnight.

By morning, the patient was his old self again, ie suffering from spinal subdural haematoma. In the post-clinical discussion, no clear explanation emerged, but the fact that the teapot had once stood on a shelf next to a garlic plant (a vital fact not previously known to the surgical team) was held to be of prime significance.

Twinkle, Twinkle

As I expected, thousands of you have written to ask if the decision by *Blue Peter* superstar Valerie Singleton to leave the BBC had anything to do with Russia's simultaneously launching a giant mirror into space, and of course it had. No flies on you, you know Russia is broke, how could they possibly afford it, you said, and when you turned on the news and saw the object in question, you immediately twigged.

The Znamya satellite was constructed by Valerie from 500 old cocoa tins, three miles of flex recycled from defunct Christmas tree lights, the tin foil from five million milk-bottle tops sent in by schoolkids, and glue made by rendering down hundreds of animals which had appeared on *Blue Peter* and subsequently been put by in case they might one day come in useful.

Valerie is now working full-time at the Moscow Space Institute, where sources tell me that she is planning to put an airship in orbit around Mars, as soon as viewers come up with enough bin-liners.

A Short History of Romance

2,000,000,000 BC
Unicellular life appears. An amoeba, it reproduces by parthenogenesis, involving no partner. It is therefore pretty happy, especially as nobody asks it where it has been all night.

30,000,000 BC
Earliest apes appear. This is Oligocene period (from Greek, meaning 'few'), and a handful of apes thus have great time, since you can lope for weeks without meeting ape of opposite sex, which means that when you do, both parties are extremely grateful. Ugly apes have as much fun as attractive ones, and do not have to stay in every night washing their hair. As a result, however, apes naturally begin to proliferate, so that within less than six million years some apes are starting to get choosy. Thus, the more repulsive apes take to trying to hang on to their mates permanently, in case chance doesn't come again. It is the dawn of matrimony.

1,700,000 BC Earliest known humans appear. Hunting and food-gathering begin. Shift in pair-bonding pattern emerges, since females who can make lizard tasty gain edge over females with good legs.

400,000 BC Homo Erectus stage. Human beings stand up, and body hair thins, as the result of which big busts become more

evident. Pair-bonding pendulum swings away from lizard cuisine.

350,000 BC Date of Heidelberg jaw. From size and elaborate hinge work, palaeontologists have now been able to sex it with confidence, also attribute to it beginnings of domestic conversation, eg 'What time do you call this, I have been slaving over this bloody lizard crumble all day, I was given to understand you were out gathering snails, how long does that take, I bet you've been lurching around after that top-heavy slag up the cliff, what is that curly red hair doing on your club, I have not given you the best years of my life just so some . . .'

350,000 BC (*later the same evening*) Date of Heidelberg headache.

200,000 BC Discovery of fire. It is now possible to get a decent steak. New area of marital discord is ushered in, since it is even more possible to get a lousy steak.

80,000 BC Neanderthal period. Tools become more sophisticated: the needle is refined, making it possible to invent the nightdress. Cohabitation enters darkest phase to date.

50,000 BC First Ice Age. Neanderthal man — insisting it was Neanderthal woman's job to get firewood

in, bloody hell must I do every little thing myself, and while we're on about it, it wouldn't kill your mother to get up off her backside once in a while — becomes extinct.

30,000 BC Emergence of Cro-Magnon man. Cave painting begins, along with violent arguments about what colour to do dining room. As chisels develop, Cro-Magnon woman asks for shelf to be put up in kitchen.

18,000 BC Last Ice Age. Cro-Magnon man reckons it is hardly worth putting up shelf now, and becomes extinct.

12,000 BC Rise of Proto-Neolithic civilization. Wheel invented. Wife not allowed to roll it.

3500 BC Sumerian civilization flourishes. Cuneiform writing invented, radically changing whole nature of romance, since it is now possible to write notes saying: 'I miss you my darling, when is that ratfaced husband of yours going on nights again, SWALK.' As it is also possible to find them lying around in pockets, a new vitality enters married life, together with major surgery.

3000 BC Cretan civilization. First recorded example of bridegroom saying: 'It is a small thing,

but Minoan.' Period is also remarkable for rise of gold and silver ornamentation: sweet dish invented, and becomes first example of an item made not for using but for giving. Such is glut of production that weddings alone will not mop up flood, thus engagement party is invented. This is so successful a marketing operation, it allows goldsmiths and silversmiths to diversify into cruet sets.

2000 BC Abraham leads the great emigration from Mesopotamia into Canaan, but it does not help, his mother-in-law finds out where he is from the butcher.

1988 BC God commands Abraham to slay his son Isaac. His mother-in-law commands him to make the boy a solicitor. It is no contest: by 1982 BC, Isaac has eight junior partners, plus a branch in Hebron specializing in corporate finance.

1184 BC Menelaus goes to Sparta on business, and while he is away, Paris comes in to service dishwasher. He then persuades dishwasher to elope with him to Troy, whereupon the Greeks lay siege to it. Siege lasts 10 years, which means that although Helen was undoubtedly the world's most beautiful woman at the start, by the end she is lying third, behind Miss

Guatemala and Julia Morley. Menelaus takes Helen back to Sparta, but sees a lot of Miss Guatemala on the side.

753 BC Rhea Silvia, mother of Romulus and Remus, takes part-time job in a Latium boutique, but has nowhere to leave twins. She asks an agency for a nanny, but, due to a typing error, they send her a wolf. It does not matter, the wolf is very good with kids, and also a stickler for tidiness; anyone leaving toys around is liable to lose a leg. In consequence, Romulus and Remus grow up right, and found Rome. Dr Spock may have known a thing or two, but he wasn't in the wolf's league.

46 BC Carpet containing Cleopatra delivered to Julius Caesar. Cleopatra: 'Have you told her yet?' Caesar: 'She hasn't been feeling very well lately.' First recorded example of this popular exchange.

0 BC Breakthrough in attitude to one-parent families.

AD 60 Boadicea fits sword blades to her chariot wheels, leaves pitiful trail of new

Roman sopranos in her wake. Later, she edits *Spare Rib*.

618 Foundation of T'ang Dynasty, ushering in 128-piece dinner service. This revolutionizes marriage, since only way anybody can afford one is to have big formal do with 128 guests, and wedding list at Harrods.

663 Synod of Whitby installs Roman Christianity in Britain, causing countless problems, least of which is that very few people can spell 'rhythm'.

868 Earliest printed book appears, in China. However, since several hundred couples suffer serious damage atttempting page 32, book is quickly withdrawn.

879 Following Danish invasion, King Alfred seeks refuge in peasant woman's hut. Her husband, who has been asleep in garden, is woken by smell of a neglected oven, but proves an inferior swordsman to the king. This comes as no surprise to his wife.

1000 Leif Ericsson discovers America. He is met on beach by a tall woman with wonderful teeth

who is prepared to enter into a meaningful one-on-one mutual life experience in which both partners respect one another's space. Ericsson gets back in his boat.

1066 Normans introduce contraceptive to Britain. It is called garlic.

1099 Crusades, or I Have To Go Abroad On Business. Hardly surprising English force fares so badly: of 18,400 crusaders who set out, 9,200 are secretaries, and only a handful get further than Brighton.

1327 Bad year for marriage; Edward II comes out of closet. Since he is subsequently killed with red-hot poker, it is also a bad year for coming out of closets.

1536 Execution of Anne Boleyn radically changes English sexual mores. Husbands are encouraged to believe that it is no longer necessary to bring home bunches of daffs or engage in enervating foreplay; all you do is put an axe on bedside table. Women, however, respond by waiting for

1558, when Elizabeth I introduces fashion for virgin spinsterhood. There is practically no sex to be had anywhere, which is particularly tough on Sir Walter Raleigh, who has just invented the cigarette for afterwards, and was hoping to clean up.

1590 Shakespeare, and full flowering of English drama. Hardly have people begun marrying again than they have to start going to the theatre all the time. In arguments about who had the tickets, where to park horses, who fell asleep during first act, whether to eat before or after, whose turn it is to take baby-sitter home, thousands die.

1669 Nell Gwyn.

1993 Hack's wife bursts in, inquiring whether hack realizes it is now 3 am, not of course that it is a question of hack choosing between her and typewriter, hack cries for God's sake, I have only got to 1669 and not even touched on rubberwear or politicians yet, wife says what is hack writing about, hack says romance my darling, hack's wife goes ha bloody ha.

A Guinea Pig Writes

Dear Sir,

I turn to you in my hour of need, I am at my wits' end, which is not far to go if you are a guinea pig (we were not at the front of the queue when the big brains were being handed out. About the only things behind us were headlice, amoebae, and the Board of British Rail.)

Nevertheless, this does not mean we can be mucked about. It is bad enough being held up by the tail every five minutes so's kids can see if your eyes fall out, without being treated like something the cat's dragged in (and I do not use the phrase lightly, I speak as something the cat has frequently dragged in, and it is no joke, I can tell you, it does not half bring the roses to your cheeks.) Where was I? Oh, yes, British Rail.

A few days ago, I heard that BR were looking for guinea pigs to be tied to poles alongside Intercity tracks to gauge the effects of having trains belt past at 140 mph, so I thought, why not, there could be a bob or two in this, possibly a free Awayday to Rhyl, so I applied, and they said, all right, turn up at the designated Bath–Swindon section at 9 am on Wednesday, bringing spare underwear and P45.

But when I got there there was nobody about, only this chalked notice saying that, due to staff shortages, the experiment would now take place outside Macclesfield on Friday. Do not ask how I got to Macclesfield, but when I did there was just these poles lying around and a bloke with a portable phone saying: 'Look, I do not care what it says on your bloody chit, these are the wrong kind of poles, these are 10-foot non-ferrous self-tapping, what is required are 12-foot concrete-bedded steel as per ours of the 14th ultimo . . .'

So I went up to this other bloke in a cap and he said: 'I am a porter, you cannot speak to me without an appointment.' So I waited for about three hours and eventually a woman with a microphone announced something but God knows what it was, she was probably attempting to talk guinea pig but, whatever it was, everyone else clocked off.

After a bit a train came by and stopped and I was going to get on it just to be out of the rain, but then the windows opened and there were all these mad-eyed, unshaven people screaming: 'Is this Surbiton, we have been redirected, we have been on this train for two days, there is no heating, there is no buffet car,' and I thought, I am not getting on that, I could get eaten.

That was four days ago. I am outside Didcot now. They have got the right poles, but the ropes to tie us on have gone to Aberdeen due to signal failure at Crewe. I shall have to pack this in, I do not know why I got involved in the first place, I should have stayed at home running around inside my wheel, it may not do 140 but it takes me there and it brings me back.

Yours etc

Windsorus Rex . . .

While I am of course delighted that the Princess of Wales has finally decided to allow her two young sons to see *Jurassic Park*, I nevertheless remain puzzled over her initial worries that the film might frighten them out of their little wits. Of all the countless millions of children who are about to be plunged into a world populated by peculiar creatures from a prehistoric era which have somehow managed against all the odds to survive into the twentieth century, I can think of none less likely to find it unfamiliar than Prince William and Prince Harry.

Stand by Your Beds!

Before the whingeing leftist layabouts of our something-for-nothing society put in their two penn'orth (which itself they would not have, of course, were it not for the generosity of our caring Government), may I say how wholeheartedly I support the wonderful new Sickfare scheme?

For those who missed this morning's announcement, Sickfare is the Downing Street policy unit's characteristically enlightened plan to allow those citizens lucky enough to be benefiting from the National Health Service to do their bit for the economy, instead of just lounging about in hospital, wolfing costly drugs, wrinkling precious laundry, expecting expensive staff to spend all day cutting, stitching, and running about with bedpans, blithely consuming the country's limited resources of bottled blood, new joints, spare organs, artificial limbs and so forth, and generally living the life of Riley.

Or, in some cases, the death of Riley, thereby putting a further burden on the balance sheet, at untold risk to Mrs Bottomley's chances of becoming Prime

They've put me in charge of VAT returns. The irony is, that's why I needed the frontal lobotomy in the first place

Minister or, indeed, Queen.

Now, there are currently 346,000 patients loafing in hospital beds, of whom a good 90 per cent can sit up, and an astonishing 62 per cent actually hobble about a bit.

Vast numbers of these leisured folk, moreover, either are, or once were, workers in all manner of trades, industries and professions, *yet none of them presently does a hand's turn!*

Under Sickfare's enlightened no-work-no-cure provisions, however, patients would be organized into working co-operatives, which is to say that wards would no longer be designated obstetric, orthopaedic, geriatric, and so on, they would instead accommodate patients according to skill — carpenters, boilermakers, vets, tailors, solicitors, etc — and operations would be conducted on a bulk rota system, to maximize teamwork potential. Thus, in the time it takes to recover from, say, their hernia operations, one wardful of 30 men could build an articulated lorry, another wardful could be checking the Tesco VAT returns, a third developing the holiday snaps of a town the size of Huddersfield, and so on.

All profits generated would, of course, go to the Exchequer, and be placed in the capable hands of Mr Clarke. For, surely, if a welfare state cannot benefit by state welfare, then who can?

Coming soon: Schoolfare, or how to get three A-levels while working up a chimney.

A Cod Writes

Dear Sir,

I think I speak for all of us up the Dogger Bank when I say that the cod is slow to anger. It takes a lot to get a cod's dander up. Down the long arches of the years, the cod has uncomplainingly subjected itself to all manner of suffering and degradation in the service of man, without once giving a thought to retaliation; it has never even crossed our minds to deep-fry men in batter, re-arrange them as man fingers, serve their eggs on toast, or extract man-liver oil. That is not our way.

We have also served and suffered in two world wars, without any recognition. You hear a lot about submarine menace, but there is never any reference to what it did to cod, people go on about torpedoes and depth charges and so forth missing their mark, but they never missed their mark as far as cod were concerned, they always blew up somewhere, and where they blew up there was always cod, we did our bit all right, but when was the last time you saw a monument to The Unknown Cod?

We do not bang on about any of this, though; ours not to reason why, ours but to end up in cheese sauce, we know our place in the food chain. Or did. Not now. If you were watching the news last Monday, you will have seen a French fisherman clouting a gendarme with a British cod. I hope you will not have believed your eyes, I hope you will have said to yourself, stone me, that British cod gave its life for this country, it got itself plucked from the bosom of its family, gutted, decapitated, frozen, and shipped off to France to do its bit for the balance of payments, instead of which it has ended up being booted all over some Frog bloody warehouse before being shovelled onto some Frog bloody tip, this calls for retaliation, it is time to start bunging Golden Delicious in the skip.

But has there been a peep out of John Selwyn Gummer? Has there hell, he is no doubt up his elegant premises sluicing his foie gras down with a nice full Burgundy prior to slicing himself a chunk of Camembert, do not talk to me about bloody Maastricht, a bloke I know had this English lamb in the back of his cab the other day, but don't even ask what he told me, I wouldn't know where to begin.

Yours etc

Medicine Balls

Because so many thrilled and excited people have written to Virginia Bottomley inquiring as to how her wonderful new hospital league tables will work, she has asked me to help her by drafting a brief explanation here, so that at least *Sunday Express* readers will stop pestering her; she is a busy Minister, she has simple but elegant little suits to get tailored, she has discreet but effective highlights to get put in, she has sensible but foxy shoes to get chosen, she cannot be everywhere at once.

Basically, then, the Benson & Tetley NHS League will comprise four divisions, embracing 88 major hospitals. Smaller hospitals will compete in various regional minor leagues, the leaders of which will, at the end of each year, enter a sudden-death play-off, from which the two hospitals with the fewest sudden deaths will go into the Fourth Division to replace its two relegated hospitals. The points will be awarded according to National Health Association rules, eg, 1 point for an admission, 2 for a diagnosis, 3 for a correct diagnosis, 4 for providing drugs, 5 for providing the right drugs, 6 for an operation, 7 for a successful operation, and so on. Set against these will be numerous penalties for minor infringements, such as wrong leg off, and major ones, such as right leg off but wrong patient, with yellow and red cards for really serious professional fouls, such as both legs off man who only came in to read the meter.

The Benson & Tetley League Competition is not, of course, to be confused with the Norwich Rumbelow Hospital Cup. This is an open competition for all hospitals, including non-league and amateur, which will give keen but minor healthworkers, eg, veterinary students, school matrons, witch doctors, Cubs with first-aid badges, and so on, the chance to have a go at NHS patients who have been on waiting-lists for so long they are more than willing to let someone take a stab at their hernia with a penknife.

Does all this, many of you inquired, have anything to do with that other enlightened piece of legislation, the National Lottery? Yes, it does. Very soon, the Government, in association with Littlehills Pools, will be sending out coupons to enable millions of you to bet on hospital results. Which means that each week, for an outlay of less than a pound, the half-dozen or so lucky punters who have correctly forecast eight NHS hospital points-tallies will carry off the staggering prize of an entirely free operation, on immediate demand, at the private hospital of their choice.

Man Coming Round to Silly Point

It may be that my genius has become delirious through getting up at 4 am every day to watch the most horrible television in the world, but I rather believe that I can help Michael Howard in the matter of juvenile criminals. He does not know what to do with them. He does not know where to put them. He does not know what will become of them.

He has not been watching the Test matches. Had he, like me, sat staring in glum disbelief as England's clapped-out wrinklies were given a right seeing-to by players half their ages, it might perhaps have occurred to him that what our national side most conspicuously lacked was not the inability to do much except shuffle somewhere between back and front foot, bowl off a length, and moan about the food, the beds, the weather, the pitches, the umpires, and everything else, what they most conspicuously lacked was menace, hostility, and the sheer native will to wreak maximum havoc upon whatever they came across.

Since the only place you will currently find such commitment in the British is among our teenage criminals, Mr Howard's course seems to me obvious. Never mind new chokeys, more policing, heavier sentences, or the, what was it, reassertion of family values, what this country needs to introduce is cricket borstals. Young offenders would be committed to these for not less than five years, during which time they would spend all day channelling their anti-social aggression into hurling the ball and wielding the bat, under such expert tutelage as may be imported from other cricketing nations.

Healthier, happier, cheaper, more practical, and potentially far more nationally beneficial than any other penal option, this scheme could well be, quite literally, a winner. Provided, of course, that nobody lets Ted Dexter within a mile of it.

Oh, When the Saints . . .

It is reported that His Holiness John Paul II, who has already sanctioned the canonization of more saints than any other pope in living memory, is about to create several more. If you have wondered how on earth, in this day and age, he manages to find so many worthy candidates, wonder no more:

ST TRACY OF BRENTFORD

The Patron Saint of Skincare

In 1987, at the tender age of 17, Tracy was beyond any question the loveliest teenager in all Essex. In the course of that year alone, she had been voted Miss Scrap Metal, Miss Fur Dice, Miss Jacuzzi, Miss Gravel Pit, Miss Up-And-Over Garage Door, and Miss Floodlit Patio, primarily on the strength of her flawless complexion. Because of this, she was then bombarded with irresistibly lucrative offers to model various ranges of high-profile skincare products, including Zitzap, Pimplene, Greasegun, Spotsmash, Bristlette, Boilblast, Wartola, and, of course, Nosqueeze Pour Elle, as the result of which attention, between 1988 and 1990, her face fell off, whereupon the Blessed Tracy immediately died of exposure. Every Whit Monday since, the impressive Romford statue erected in her memory sprouts hundreds of blackheads which are then miraculously removed by local nuns using only soap and water.

ST BRIAN OF WILLESDEN

The Patron Saint of Viewing

On the morning of 18 September 1979, Brian Kenneth Foskett, one of South Willesden's most prominent caretakers, sat down in front of his newly purchased television set to watch *Postman Pat*. He did not move from the spot until 21 April 1988, when the set finally overheated and blew up, burning down 14a Mafeking Villas, and Brian Kenneth Foskett.

Thus, for almost nine years, the Blessed Brian had forsaken family, friends, work and everything else, surviving only on his unemployment pittance and daily visits from Meals-on-Wheels (his wife having left him in 1983 and run off to Bangladesh with a man who had come in to adjust the aerial), in order to devote himself totally to viewing everything which the Almighty, in his infinite wisdom, had caused to be placed before him.

During all that time, he was never heard to utter one single word of complaint or criticism, even though there were long stretches of his lonely round-the-clock vigil when he had absolutely nothing to stare at except test cards, static interference, or Jeremy Beadle.

Never before has the love that asks no questions been quite so egregiously manifested; it is said that at board meetings of both the BBC and ITV, when agonizing worries about plummeting programme standards beset the assembled executives, the spectral figure of the Blessed Brian materializes noiselessly above their table to bring them solace and reassurance.

THE FORTY MARTYRS OF KYOTO

The Patron Saints of Export

Collectively known as St Gramoflex & Co Ltd, the Forty Blessed Martyrs were originally a sales delegation sent, early in 1985, from Slough Trading Estate to the Far East in an incredibly courageous attempt to interest the Japanese in a range of British transistor radios.

Ridiculed, scorned, abused, and on more than one occasion put in strait-jackets for what was deemed to be their own good, they nevertheless pressed on selflessly with their door-to-door mission, but finally succeeded only in selling their hats to a Nagasaki fisherman who immediately flooded the world with cheap imitation synthetic bowlers, and retired to Palm Springs.

Unable to raise the return fare, the Forty Martyrs set up a makeshift office in a bat-infested cave outside Kyoto, occupying their time and keeping their spirits up by sending optimistic memos in triplicate to one another until malnutrition at last took its inevitable toll. Every year, an empty order book is ceremonially burned at the magnificent Board of Trade urinal erected in their memory, and departmental prayers taken from Heseltine Ancient & Modern are offered up for the miraculous failure of all foreign economies.

ST KEVIN OF INTERPRAT EXPRESS

The Patron Saint of Hedgehogs

On the dark, freezing morning of 15 December 1990, young motorbike

messenger Kevin Shellsuit, without a second thought for his own safety (or indeed for anything else), pluckily set out, in thick fog, down icy roads, on bald tyres and with no silencer, to break the world record for delivering a box of typewriter ribbons from Shepherds Bush to Ludgate Circus.

That world record, which before Kevin's astonishing run had stood at an impressive nine sideswiped cars, two dismembered cyclists, six dead dogs, and an entire bus queue required to take early retirement, was resoundingly beaten by a margin of four old age pensioners, three gravel-bins, and half a police horse.

Tragically, while making his return journey down the oncoming fast lane of the Hammersmith Flyover, the Blessed Kevin martyred himself against a 40-ton articulated juggernaut, whose driver, noticing no more than a slight bump, carried on to Felixstowe.

The saint's holy remains were scattered all over East Anglia as they fell piecemeal from the tyre-treads, hence his patronage.

ST GREGORY OF WOLDMAN ROBBINS, JELKS, SPANIER, GIBLING

The Patron Saint of Advertising

Dogged for more years than he cared to remember by countless products wholly unworthy of his unflaggingly dedicated copywriting — Greemley's Miracle Liniment, whose side-effects introduced bubonic plague to Dundee; the Norbling Drip-Dry One-Piece Pyjama, which strangled the then Home Secretary; the Anglo-Zambian Airbus, which crashed and blew up inside its hangar; Black & Crosswell's Patent Depilatory Soup, held responsible for a spate of still-inexplicable pregnancies among senior officers of the Household Cavalry — the Blessed Gregory decided to devote his latter years to publicizing the cause of Plaid Cymru, who, when

they failed to win the General Election, martyred him, unspeakably, with a sharpened leek. After his death, miraculous rises in the sales of all the products with which he had been associated brought copywriters from all over the world to touch his coffin, particularly on 18 March when a bedsheet washed in water to which a miracle ingredient (a drop of the Saint's sweat) has been added turns grey and falls to bits.

ST BERYL OF TORREMOLINOS

The Patron Saint of Package Holidays

In August 1959, an Englishwoman bound for Zurich but put on the wrong aircraft by a travel agent who went bust the moment she was airborne, found herself stranded on what was then the undeveloped wasteland of the Costa Brava. Local peasants took pity on her, because she waved money at them, and put her up in a partially built hut, fed her on bowls of rancid rice

with prawns' heads in, let her paddle in the local sewer, got her drunk on an expensive local wine made from old torch batteries, pinched any exposed flesh they could find, and when she expressed an interest in souvenirs, gave her a castanet held together with Sellotape, in return for her wallet. Throughout the fortnight she spent with them, however, the Blessed Beryl never stopped smiling, because she believed you always had to look on the bright side and worse things happened at sea, a philosophy which enabled her, when she finally struggled back to England, to phone all her friends to tell them what a lovely holiday she'd had, she couldn't recommend the place too highly. She then unpacked, and died of gastroenteritis.

The rest is history, and since it succeeded in convincing the entire Spanish population that miracles can indeed happen, the Pope of course had no option but instant canonization.

Aux Armes, Citoyens!

As a passionate democrat, I am naturally delighted that the honours system is to be given over into the hands of the people, so that henceforth you and I will be able to fax a simple form to 10 Downing Street, nominating the hero of our choice for gong or ermine.

Even as I applaud it, however, I have to say that John Major's ongoing commitment to yielding more power to the citizenry does not ongo far enough. A wonderful democratic opportunity has been missed; but fortunately (did you guess?), I am here to make that omission good.

The time has come for a Dishonours System to be introduced, on terms exactly similar to those just proposed. For far too long, far too many of those who enjoy unmerited rank and authority have been getting away scot-free with ineptitude, corruption, unsavoury behaviour, and permutations of all these and more, without the nation's citizenry having any say in the matter, because the mutual backscratching system which elevated these rotters further ensures that they are kept elevated. The rest of us, to whom they frequently do great damage, can do no more than stand idly by while iffy judges, crackpot bishops, greedy bankers, dingbat politicians, clueless industrialists, and nitwit nobs of every shape and size enjoy status and privileges to which they have no entitlement whatever. This must cease forthwith, to which democratic end I have prepared a simple form for citizens to cut out, fill in, and fax immediately to 10 Downing Street:

Dear Prime Minister,

I should like the undermentioned public ratbag to be:

(a) Stripped of all honours ☐ titles ☐ positions ☐

(b) Invited to Buckingham Palace to be kicked round Palace Yard by HM the Queen ☐

(c) Thrown off Beachy Head ☐

(d) All of the above ☐

Ratbag's name _____

My name _____

A Megastar Writes

Dear Sir,

I have been shaken to my very wossname by this week's news that because of the rapid rise and spread of video surveillance, legislation is to be introduced to ensure that recordings made by security cameras are not allowed to fall into hands that might exploit them for profit. This legislation is not merely a public outrage, it is a blow from which my personal ambitions may never recover.

For some years now, I have spent a great deal of time and effort in preparing myself for a major television career. I am already famous in my local Tesco's, where security staff say it is always a pleasure watching me choosing the right catsmeat or wondering whether I can get my trolley through a particularly tricky gap in Special Offer pyramids, shaking my head, scratching my chin, rolling my eyes etc etc, they say I am one of a kind, and the man down the off-licence told me it really makes his day when I dance in covered with Cherry Blossom and singing 'Sonny Boy' at his ceiling, it is such a change from everyone just walking across his screen, picking up a six-pack, and walking back, they do not have the first idea.

Similarly, whenever I go on holiday, I always put something entertaining in my suitcase, eg, hand grenade or human skull, so's it gets picked up on the scanner, plus walking stiff-legged so's they think I have a shotgun down my trousers, it is not going too far to say that I am already something of a top screen celebrity up Gatwick.

Not to mention such comedy classics as *Me Filling up Tank and Hopping about with Petrol All Over My Feet*, *Me Nearly Turning Somersault up the Lloyds Cashpoint*, *Me Running into the Building Society with a Balaclava on and Getting Everybody to Lie on the Floor While I Do Card Tricks*, and hundreds more.

I did all this because it was only a matter of time before the BBC pulled *Eldorado* and started looking around for something better, at which point I would have been in there like a ferret, but it is all over now, it is goodbye Tinseltown, do not look for me next time you're in Rumbelows, I am getting out of show business for good.

Yours etc

Happy Days Are Here Again!

May I just say how wholeheartedly I concur with the Prime Minister's exhortation to us not to talk Britain down? Personally, wherever I look, I see nothing but cause for national rejoicing.

There are now, for example, over 3,000,000 Britons who are no longer required to get out of a nice warm bed every morning and trudge off to some ghastly boring job.

Sympathetically lengthened NHS waiting-lists mean that huge numbers of fortunate people are not being summarily dragged off to hospitals for terrifying operations, while for every lucky youngster currently attending a school wisely teaching him not enough to get into what would otherwise be overcrowded universities, there is another equally lucky one not going

to school at all but instead teaching himself to drive all manner of cars, climb all manner of drainpipes, and pick all manner of locks, thereby standing himself in wonderful stead for the adult life to come.

That these youngsters give almost no trouble to the police is proved by the encouraging drop in arrests, but what is even more encouraging is that even those arrested, of whatever age, are likely to be freed either for lack of safe evidence or by judges trained not to know what day it is, so that they may be returned to the community to live happily ever after, just like the senile or mentally disturbed who no longer have to be isolated and discriminated against in institutions but can now live like anybody else who has the price of a cardboard box.

Which brings me to the economic miracle whereby the price of housing is coming down faster and faster, thanks to a remarkably far-sighted policy of linking negative equity to repossession, with its further boon of strengthening family values by putting everyone in the same room! Where they are perfectly content to stay, counting their blessings that they cannot afford to buy cars which could well do irreparable damage to an environment now beginning to improve thanks to the lack of pollution from wisely closed industries, and that they do not need to save up to go anywhere on shrewdly overpriced trains which would only dump them somewhere else anyway, because of the astute use of the wrong sort of drizzle.

Truly, we have never had it so good!

A Pig Writes

Dear Sir,

I turn to you as a philosopher of some standing, you that is, not me, you do not get a lot of time for philosophy up a pig farm, take your eye off the trough for a bit of a think and before you can say Jack Wittgenstein there is a row of snouts in it like a brick bloody wall, you cannot get back in, it is goodbye dinner. That is due to our profession, we are in the fattening business, we never stop, it is what pigs do. Or did. You will know whereof I speak, it is last week's British Medical Association welcome for the transgenic pig. You will have seen that it is now possible to grow human-type organs in pigs, due to where human genes get injected into a sow's fertilized eggs and when the piglets grow up they are full of odds and ends for transplanting into humans. Now, do not get me wrong, I have nothing against a pig's organs ending up inside a human, they do that already, I am all in favour of donating a nice pair of devilled kidneys or a nice bit of grilled liver, that is my job, it is why I spend all day fattening, take that away and what is my life for, it is important and rewarding work; you never know, I could end up in the Savoy Grill, I could find myself on a royal fork, you can go right to the top in this business, all you need is a bit of luck.

No, what bothers me are two other aspects which the BMA has not addressed, and, believe me, both of them spell trouble. The first is where a new race of donor-pigs is bound to introduce class distinction into pig society, we are looking at two-tier pigs here, with most of us ending up in Dewhurst's but a chosen few ending up in Bart's. We shall have these flash pigs poncing about and banging on about being human on their mother's side and how they are not going to get a seeing-to from a butcher's cleaver, they are not going to end up as two gross of bangers up some works' canteen, they are going to get scalpelled by a top surgeon, possibly a knight, they will depart this life in some posh hospital, could be private, weeping nurses round them, all that. They will make my life a misery.

But even worse, from your point of view, is that pig-breeding is a funny old game, you wouldn't credit what goes on after lights out, and your average farmer does not have eyes in the back of his head, never mind not always being able to tell one pig from another. You know what I am saying here, I am saying that the day may not be far off when you sit down for breakfast and, after a bit, you say to your wife, here, this kidney tastes peculiar, and she says, funny you should say that, this liver's not all it should be, and the reason is you are eating what is, genetically speaking, some bloke in Doncaster.

Philosophize on that, sunshine!

Yours etc

God Save the Loophole!

Ever since Thursday's statement by Buckingham Palace that the Queen was exempt, 'by reason of her special position,' from the law requiring her subjects to wear a rear seatbelt, thousands of you have rung this office with inquiries concerning other special dispensations which Her Majesty alone enjoys. Having now researched the matter fully, I am in a position to publish the complete list.

Travel: Her Majesty is uniquely entitled to stand upstairs on buses. Should she spit, however, she is liable to the same fine as anyone else. She is also allowed to lean her bicycle against shop windows. When flying, she is not permitted to get up before the plane has come to a complete halt, but she does not have to take care when opening the overhead lockers. On trains, she is allowed to smoke in the lavatories, though not pipes or cigars. On the underground, she may not go up a down escalator, or vice-versa, but she is allowed to jump over the barrier if she hears her Tube train coming, provided she has a valid ticket for the journey.

Sport: When bowling, Her Majesty is allowed to deliver more than one bouncer per over, except in one-day matches, but she must observe the new dress codes and not wear a headscarf when batting or fielding. She is also, when playing in goal, permitted to move before a penalty is struck, and would not normally be sent off for bad language, unless violence was involved. Should her opponent go down during a boxing match, Her Majesty is not required to walk to a neutral corner.

Shopping: While Her Majesty is allowed to go through the checkout marked '6 items or less' with 7 items or more, no special dispensation applies regarding taking the trolley from the shop. In post offices, staff may not ask her to go to the next counter, and in garages she does not have to switch off the engine while filling up, though she must take the cigarette out of her mouth. She is allowed to bring her dog into foodshops, but if it widdles against anything, she is not exempt from prosecution.

Driving: In addition to the seatbelt dispensation, Her Majesty is allowed to hoot after 11 pm and overtake in the Blackwall Tunnel. If parked on a double yellow line, however, she is liable to be towed away, but only by a peer of the realm.

Thanks for the Memory

I was intrigued by Wednesday's report, or possibly Thursday's, hang on, I tell a lie, it was the day the man came to fix the, the, oh God, big white thing, you put clothes in, it goes round and round, anyway I read this report in the, in the, no I didn't, that's right, I was in the car, I was driving towards, oh God, that little town on the river where they, where they, I think it has a cathedral, no it hasn't, it has a, what are those places where they train fish, never mind, I was going there in the car and I, wait a minute, I wasn't going there at all, I was coming back from seeing dear old, dear old, bloody hell, tall man, little ginger beard, he looks a bit like the actor in that series on, is it Channel 4, he plays a, a, it isn't a detective, it's more of a, dear God, I can see him now, I know him like the back of my, of my,

correction, I didn't hear it on the radio at all, I saw it on the box, I was having a quick one in the Dog and, and, those birds that talk, it's on the tip of my, wait a sec, it might have been the Queen's Thingy, I couldn't swear, it's where the barmaid has a very small, er, no it's not, the barmaid with the very small whateveritis works at the Duke of, the Duke of, it'll come to me in a minute, unless of course I'm mixing her up with the checkout girl at Sainsbury's, it could well be, if Sainsbury's is the one where they do the, the, anyway, the point is that this report said that people who drink coffee have better memories than people who don't and I thought what a load of old cobblers, look at me, I never touch the stuff, and there's nothing wrong with my, with my, oh you know, I said it just now, that thing in your head.

No Monkey Business

Now that Ola the chimpanzee, whose random selection of shares in Swedish public companies thumpingly outperformed the alternative choices made by the country's leading investment experts, has walked off with the title of 'Sweden's Top Financial

Adviser', I can see nothing to prevent his going on to a hugely successful career in that normally fraught and iffy profession.

For not only is Ola self-evidently as incorruptible as he is clever, I am also given to understand that the only toes he ever wants to suck are this own.

Help Yourself!

I was overjoyed last week to note the short shrift the Prime Minister gave to all those moaning minnies who have been banging on about the Government's lack of a coherent energy policy. The levelling of VAT on home heating fuel, he declared, could be more than offset if people would only roll up their sleeves and lag their lofts.

This is leadership of the first water. Nor, now that the wind is in his sails, will it stop there, as those of us with access to authoritative sources can happily testify.

Take, for example, the imminent White Paper from his radiant Health Secretary: entitled 'Whither the NHS?', and subtitled 'Wither the NHS!', it is packed with invaluable advice brilliantly calculated to see off her critics. Did you know, for example, that 40 per cent of all dental problems could be cured by a piece of string and a doorknob, or that a survey of malingerers claiming to need glasses showed that the vast majority had never thought of asking someone to tell them which bus was coming, or, once aboard, whether there was anything interesting in the paper? And I think we shall have heard the last complaint about the ambulance service, once the chapter entitled 'Nothing wrong with your thumb, is there?' has shown layabouts how easy it is to hitch-hike to their nearest hospital. The document is full of invaluable tips on

everything from learning to limp efficiently to how to shout at the deaf, and I would draw special attention to the Appendix, illustrating how it can be taken out using only a mirror and a penknife.

The Bottomley proposals might well be upstaged, mind, by the new Home Office Law & Order booklet in which Mr Howard shows citizens how to whittle a combined truncheon and whistle from an old cricket stump, thwart burglars by boarding up their windows, reduce car theft by selling their cars, and substantially cut mugging and other assaults by having the sheer common sense not to go out.

These, indeed, are all points also taken up by the Education Secretary in his new policy document showing how parents who stay at home and use a truncheon can teach their children to read and do simple sums, with the added benefit that boarded-up windows will stop those children getting out and assaulting schoolteachers or joyriding in cars that people haven't had the wit to sell.

Should, however, these latter continue to insist on literally going their own way, it would be unkind of me not to draw their attention to the Secretary of Transport's forthcoming Green Paper, 'Roads: The Way Forward', and its invaluable advice on handling potholes: keep a shovel and a sack of gravel in the boot. You know it makes sense.

All the News That's Fit to Print

Following Wednesday's delivery to the Heritage Secretary of a blueprint for Press regulation, thousands of readers rang me to express their fears that this represented the thin end of state censorship. Nothing could be further from the truth.

The job of his mooted ombudsman will be to address the roots of the hardships unwarrantedly suffered by the rich and famous. Each day, crack heritage teams will be on the alert for everything from royal personages accidentally attempting to sell their snaps and stories to the highest bidder and rock stars erroneously stuffing their noses with Colombian exports, to Cabinet Ministers mistakenly scuttling off to seedy hotels under assumed names and business tycoons whose hands have somehow become caught in the corporate till. These helpless victims will be intercepted by sympathetic carers before the Press can get to them, gently relieved of mobile telephones, false moustaches, incriminating letters, tapes and members of the opposite sex to which they have unwittingly become attached, and once they have been sobered up, washed, clothed, and whatever else is required to help them conform to the standards of those in the public eye, returned to the bosoms of their families with the quiet suggestion that should they fall victim to such unfortunate disasters again, they will be crated up and deported. It is a procedure which, I am as convinced as Peter Brooke, will radically clean up our newspapers and I heartily applaud him for it.

Stands England Where It Did?

Patriots all, you will have been as overjoyed as I to learn of the great Marquess of Bath's visionary scheme to build a full-size plywood replica of Stonehenge in the grounds of Longleat, enabling Japanese tourists to kill two birds with one stone, or, indeed, three birds, given that he also plans to hold classical concerts inside it.

It has long been my contention that we demand far too much of valued visitors to these shores, carting them all over the shop in order to savour the too-far-flung treasures of our imperishable heritage and thus keeping them here for weeks when the whole thing could be done in a couple of days, thereby quadrupling foreign throughput and the sackfuls of hard currency of which we so desperately need to relieve them. Thanks to the modern miracles of polystyrene and Superglue, the whole of visit-worthy Britain could be contained in a few acres, linked to major airports by exclusive motorways and monorails and supervised by crack squads of multilingual minders who would whip the gawping jumboloads through with split-second cost-efficient timing.

Think of the hours wasted in profitlessly travelling from London to Stratford to see a long boring production of *Hamlet*, when you could be looking down from the Whispering Gallery of St Paul's into the back garden of Wordsworth's cottage where Kenneth and Emma are declaiming the Bard's most quotable bits, while behind them the Household Cavalry morris dances to Gilbert & Sullivan sung by Black Rod and the Pearly Queen from the top of the Monument. Looking for the Brontës' birthplace? First left at Canterbury Cathedral, past the Derby, sharp right at Eton, straight through Marks & Spencers, pausing only to pick up three cashmere sweaters, a length of tartan, and a roast beef and Yorkshire takeaway, then take the Brighton Belle to Westminster Abbey, cross the Serpentine by the Forth Bridge and it's just next to Madame Tussaud's, you can't miss it.

Nor should the souvenir industry be neglected. Compelled, currently, to cobble together all sorts of disparate odds and sods, how much more profitable it would be to manufacture only one: a tasteful table-lamp of the Princess of Wales, say, dressed as a Beefeater, which plays Paul McCartney's rendering of 'There'll Always Be an England' when her hat is lifted to get at the Churchill cigars inside her, and flourishing a cricket-stump with a little Nelson on the end to which is attached a useful tea-towel depicting Oliver Cromwell eating black pudding and clotted cream and reading *Winnie-the-Pooh*.

Heritage, is what we're talking here. Ask Bath. He knows. He cares.

A Flea Writes

Dear Sir,

I am a working flea, and I have been in full employment all my life, ie since last Wednesday, and yes, you are dead right, a flea does not get much of a span in this vale of tears, a flea year is equivalent to a human hour, by the time this goes to press I shall in all probability have popped my six little clogs, I shall be playing a titchy harp, unless of course I manage to get to be 100 flea years old, in which case I am still around this morning, and if Her Majesty is reading this, a telegram would not come amiss, it would crown my career, I could go to my maker on Easter Monday knowing my living had not been in vain.

Someone else will be pedalling my tiny bike by then, of course, that is the way it is in the circus world,

one door shuts, another opens, my colleague on the tightrope snuffed it a minute or so ago and before he'd hit the ground his replacement was up there with his little pole, you cannot hang about if you are a flea trainer, the show must go on. I remember — mind you, I'm going back a bit now, it must have been what, half-past ten — I was pulling our little coach round the ring and suddenly it felt heavy and I looked across and the other five were all stiffs, for a lot of fleas it is here today and gone today, but we do not

complain, we love the work, it is very varied, somersaults one minute, fencing-match the next, it is a hell of a lot better than hopping about on a dog.

Which brings me to my point. I see where Gerry Cottle is getting out of the circus business due to Animal Rights activists making his life a misery, so there is no question but that the writing is on the wall for all of us. And I do mean all: have you any idea of the consequences for the human race of suddenly having millions of fleas on the dole?

When was the last time you saw people scratching? Yes, you are not wrong, major itching has virtually died out thanks to fleas being in regular work, but if Animal Rights has its way you will all be walking around with DDT under your hats, what you have to get your esteemed readers to do is write to their MPs immediately, before it is too late, save our jobs and do your scalps a bit of good at the same time, you know it makes sense.

Yours etc

Off and Running

As one who was actually present at Aintree last weekend, I have to tell you that the new experimental rules for the Grand National worked a treat. The moment the tape lifted to neck-height to hold the horses back so that the competitors in bowler hats could start running up the course waving their red flags, I could tell that the Jockey Club, at the forefront of sporting progress as usual, was on to a winner. The punters saved a fortune in void bets, hippophile protesters cheered their heads off, and the horses were generally agreed that it was the next best thing to

being put out to stud.

My only criticism is that the experiment was so tentative. While I understand the Jockey Club's feeling that change should come slowly, after so many years of, let's face it, boring tradition, I nevertheless believe that the men in bowler hats should have been allowed to jump.

Next year, of course, they will, when their ranks, I can exclusively reveal, will be swollen to forty or fifty, and each competitor will have a flag of a different colour, and a number on his bowler hat.

Since the National is a handicap, older competitors

will be allowed to carry ladders to negotiate the more daunting fences and non-swimmers furnished with rubber rings for the water jump, while the formidable Brigadier JD 'Barmy' Duff-Guttering, who pole-vaulted for Charterhouse in the early Thirties, is determined to test National Hunt legislation to the full.

Whether injured fallers should be shot has not yet been decided, but in the opinion of all the owners, trainers, and jockeys I spoke to last Saturday, there was absolutely no question about it.

A Golly Writes . . .

Dear Sir,

I trust you will not think me, what's the word, uppity, when I say that I write in the full conviction that you will publish this letter, you are known to be a person who has nailed his liberal colours to the mast, you are an equal opportunities columnist, it is common knowledge that when the huddled masses turn up at your door yearning to be free, there is always a hot dinner on the table.

You will therefore have been very nearly as astonished and disgusted as I was to learn that I was not going to Hollywood. Despite the fact that Noddy has just been signed up for his first major feature film and will be off any minute now on the studio's Learjet, taking Big Ears, Mr Plod, Tessie Bear, and all the rest of the little simpering time-serving lickspittles with him, free in-flight Dom Perignon by the firkin, pickled prawns on sticks, personal stereo, choice of first-run movies, little red stretch pedal-limos waiting at the other end, I shall not be with them, I shall be stuck back here on my tod in the toy box, just another ethnic minority consigned to cardboard city with no job prospects.

Oh yes, they have attempted to fob you off with transparent bloody excuses about my not being politically correct, what a load of cobblers, look at Eddie Murphy, look at Bill Cosby, look at Richard Pryor, this is our time, we are big box office, and there you have it, that is the top and bottom of why Noddy and all the other disloyal little ratbags did not dig their heels in when I was passed over, that is why they did not wobble backwards and forwards outside the BBC singing 'Let My People Go!' . . . they are only too happy to drop me in it, they are scared witless I would upstage them, they are petrified I would become a megastar, and they are not wrong, I have a wonderful sense of rhythm, when my strings are going right I am a sort of black equivalent of Michael Jackson. What is left for me now? I tell you what is left for me now, the best I can hope for is a two-minute unpaid appearance in a Channel bloody 4 documentary banging on and on about how something must be done to alleviate the desperate misery of our inner nurseries.

Yours etc

Narrower Still and Narrower

I am, as you would expect, utterly appalled at the recommendation by the Royal Park Review Group that a pedestrian precinct accessed by a network of patrolled zebra crossings be created in front of Buckingham Palace so that tourists would be able to poke their heads through Her Majesty's gracious railings without getting run over.

What is this but yet another example of how this great country of ours is being forced to change its traditional ways in order to kow-tow to the demands of foreigners? It is not only outrageous that road-fund-paying patriots should be denied the opportunity of having a sporting crack at alien dimwits unable to remember which way to look when stepping off a British kerb, it is a further instance of that caring wimpishness which currently bids fair to destroy our incomparable martial heritage. I did not fight for this country in two world wars so that my children would grow up with nothing to watch but The Changing of the Lollipop Men.

Mind How You Go!

Like me, you will all, I know, have been cheered and thrilled by the proposal from the Chief Constable of South Wales that policemen should be available for private hire at £26 an hour.

I have long been a keen advocate of a system by which rich people in need of law and order could go private, since it is impeccably logical that the more property you have, the more property you will lose to unscrupulous villains eager to take it off you, and, ergo, the broader should be your rights when endeavouring to thwart them. It seems to me utterly preposterous that a multi-millionaire whose drum has just been turned over should have to stand in line for a 999 visit, a CID investigation, and the currently remote chance of an arrest and conviction, as if he were no more important than some old biddy who had been mugged for her ludicrously titchy pension.

But more even than this, they should not have to wait for the crime to be committed to enjoy the full protection the bank balance allows. Those who can afford it should be able to ring a special number whenever, say, they intend queueing at a cashpoint, or walking to the pillar box with an important letter, or going out for the evening wearing jewellery and having to park the Roller in some dark alley, whereupon two experienced policemen would arrive, immediately, one to accompany them, and the other to stay in their vacated premises. If, furthermore, their cat goes missing or the people next door are singing in the bath or a relief milkman offers them an improper suggestion, they should be able to ring up with their credit card number and be put instantly at the head of the Pending Inquiries waiting list.

Indeed, I would go further. Even when an arrest is made, it is often the case these days that an inept judge and a dumb jury will let the criminal off, accepting his defence that he found your Rembrandt in a skip. This is totally unacceptable: if you're in the lucky position of being able to afford it, you should be allowed to hire your own private judge and jury, so that the man your own private policeman has arrested will be found guilty as charged, and sent down for the term you have specified on your order form. Or, in really irritating cases, hanged by you personally: many of us would be only too happy to pay a substantial fee for the privilege.

Believe me when I say I am convinced that the Home Secretary should address the issue of private policemen as a matter of great urgency. With so many villains back on the streets as the result of the Group 4 experiment, we are none of us safe in our beds.

Probably the Worst Commercial in the World

Not nearly enough attention, in my view, was paid to last week's landmark decision by the Independent Television Commission to withdraw from our screens the Golden Wonder Pot Snacks advertisement because it brought on epileptic fits.

It was a staggering legal precedent. It was a major cultural breakthrough. It could, with any luck, change all our lives for the immeasurably better, bringing blessed relief to millions of sufferers throughout the queendom... always provided, of course, that I can count on your support. So would all readers who have had to run whimpering behind the sofa whenever the Gold Blend couple start ogling one another for the millionth time, or who have found themselves inexplicably throwing up every time Nicole and Papa do their thing with the Renault Clio, or who have suddenly broken out into sweats and trembling while watching Jeremy Beadle coughing on his mattress, please write, as soon as possible, to the ITC? Thank you.

A Tadpole Writes

Dear Sir,

I know I speak for all spawn when I say that words cannot express how thrilled I was to read in the papers that, and I quote, 'the tadpoles aboard the Columbia space shuttle are recovering.' The news can mean only one thing, ie a cure has been found for the mysterious and terrible disease which has afflicted my people since time immemorial.

Clearly, scientists have found the solution in outer space, just like they did with non-stick saucepans. They will not get back in time to save me, mind. I have had it: my tail has already wasted away, my head has begun to bulge horribly, and four peculiar growths have appeared at the corners of my body, it is the same old story, I am doomed any minute now to start hopping about uncontrollably until this brings me to the notice of the French, who will then eat me.

What has the tadpole community done to deserve this? Our behaviour is impeccable, it couldn't be much else stuck here in this bloody jelly, yet we have been singled out for this ghastly incurable affliction and nobody gives a toss, we do not see hide nor hair of Princess Diana, we never get Wembley charity concerts or national flag days, I mean, if there is a God why has it taken Him so long, He let science discover the answer to indigestion years ago, I don't call that a priority.

Yours etc

Working in Mysterious Ways

I was delighted that the rave in the nave of Winchester Cathedral was such a success, and I can only pray (if I am able to find a church which still allows that sort of thing) that the rumours of even more ambitious ecclesiastical enterprises are true. It cannot, for example, be mere coincidence, since that is not how God works, that the nave of Westminster Abbey measures exactly 60 metres, ie the length of an indoor sprinting track, and many worshippers, I know, would pay good money to watch Linford Christie going down it like the clappers (remarkably like the clappers, actually), while pole-vaulters soared above him and shot-putters and long-jumpers did their thing in either transept. Nor should the famous acoustics of St Paul's be let go to waste: there is not another venue in the country where three thousand bingo-players could convene and not miss a single call. Discussions, however, between Salisbury Cathedral and Tesco's on their brilliantly innovative Shop 'n' Pray scheme will, I fear, have to be put on a back-burner until the Government stops dragging its heels on Sunday trading legislation, but that day is not, I feel certain, far off. How could it be, when the Church of England is taking such brilliantly imaginative steps to persuade its members to halt their precipitous and preposterous flight to Rome?

A Word in Edgeways

My agent has just rung up in a state of great excitement to say that he has been asked if I would like to be a guest on Neil Kinnock's new chat show this autumn. The fee, he tells me, is quite small, but then again, I shall not be expected to say anything.

No End of a Laugh

I was much intrigued by the findings of those Liverpool sociologists whose five-year study on the prejudices of club audiences concluded, among other things, that it was only at their punchlines that racist, sexist, or obscene jokes became unacceptably offensive. Indeed, I was so intrigued that it occurred to me that there might well be a bob or two in writing a politically correct routine for the Mannings and Davidsons of this world, who would doubtless be extremely grateful to get their hands on, for example:

'Good evening, good evening, good evening! As I was coming here tonight, I was stopped, I was stopped by a Pakistani dwarf who was pushing these two Jewish fishermen along in a wheelbarrow. Excuse me, I said, excuse me, but that's the first time I've ever seen a Pakistani dwarf pushing two Jewish fishermen along in a wheelbarrow. And the Paki looked up and said: Oh, really? Which reminds me, did you hear the one about the Irish poof who went into a chemist's shop? Mind you, my wife, my wife, I'm not saying she's fat, but when she took her corset off the other day, so anyway, there was this Chinese commercial traveller, lonely country road, it's pouring with rain, pouring with rain, and all of a sudden his car runs out of petrol. So he gets out, and he can see this light, he can see this light about half a mile off, so he takes a petrol can, are you with me, he takes a petrol can, and after about ten minutes he gets to this farmhouse, he's soaked to the skin, soaked to the skin, and he bangs on the door and after a bit it opens and there's this fantastic bird, lovely long legs, all the trimmings, and she's stark naked. Stark naked!

So the commercial traveller says: Excuse me bothering you at this time of night – they're very polite, the Chinese – excuse me bothering you, but I wonder if you've got any petrol?

And she says: Don't stand out there getting drenched, come in and take your clothes off, and I'll try to find some, I'd ask my husband, but he's away on business until Thursday week. So the Chinaman says: Thank you very much – I told you he was polite – and he comes in and takes his clothes off, and after about five minutes she calls down from the bedroom, and you've been a wonderful audience, a wonderful audience, so I'd like to end with a little song, a little song entitled '*She was only a lesbian's daughter, but her name was Maureen Atkinson*,' music, maestro, if you please . . .'

Son et Loony Heir

Much as I, like you, admire Her Majesty's brave decision to contribute to the Windsor Castle restoration by throwing Buckingham Palace open to the public at £8 a shot (some might view this as demeaning, but I say it is far less so than the option of having our gracious monarch shinning up the Windsor ladder with a hod and a mouthful of nails), I am deeply disturbed that the announcement was made on the selfsame day that Prince Charles declared his conviction that such soaps as *EastEnders* and *Coronation Street* encouraged a sense of community which his mother's subjects would be wise to emulate.

They do nothing of the sort. They encourage the sense that the typical community is made up of people conspiring against one another, shrieking at one another, socking one another, and getting up to all manner of unsavoury practices likely to disaffect them from one another. I very much hope, therefore, that the Royals do not have it in mind to use the opportunity of throwing their home open to emulate what some other stately piles have on offer, ie a sound-and-light show dramatizing the family's history and personalities. Despite the fact that his misguided highness has somehow got it into his head that the example would be good for them, the public is highly unlikely to cough up £8 a nob to watch what their nightly television already offers them for nothing.

Reading in a recent DSS report that 'boredom is a major social threat', it struck me that there was an urgent need for a magazine which would help millions of people with time on their hands but no idea of what to do with it. Imagine my astonishment, therefore, when my newsagent informed me that one already existed, but very few people knew about it. Since this must rapidly be rectified, I reproduce a selection from the latest issue, in the public interest.

Or lack of it.

LOOSE END

Fairly interesting walks

Number 19: Down to the Pillar Box

Go out of the front door. Bang it. Note the little sort of ding that comes after you bang it. That is due to the bell on the door reacting to the bang.

Look at the step. The wear is the result of people walking on it. With the ruler you bought on Fairly Interesting Walks No. 14: *Up to Woolworths and Back*, measure the depth of the wear. Divide this by the number of people who have walked on the step since the house was built and it will give you the exact amount of wear each person has inflicted on the step. (You do this by the method outlined in Fairly Interesting Walks No. 9: *Going Across The Road And Looking At Your House From*

The Other Side, when we showed you how to watch your gate for people coming in and out. Following this method for seven days will give you the number of people walking on the step in a week. Simply add up the number of weeks the house has been there, and multiply by the number of people per week.)

On the front path, squat on your haunches, and watch the ants run about. Note how they can pick up a twig several times bigger than themselves. Watch them carry the twig here and there. Ants are *never* bored! Indeed, man can learn a great deal from the ant; why not see if you can find a twig several times bigger than yourself?

Then you could carry it here and there, too, for, say, 20 minutes.

From there, go out of the gate and stare at the pavement. Note how uneven it is. Retrace your steps, go back through the front door, and write to the council about the uneven pavement (40 minutes). When you have finished the letter, work out your best route to the pillar box, and discuss it with your family (two hours). Next week, we'll tell you which of you was right!

LETTERS TO THE EDITOR

Dear Sir,
I recently managed to stand three cigarettes on top of one another, and would like to meet a young woman of similar interests. I am 47, and would be prepared to travel in from Basingstoke.

Yours truly,
Eric Lamont (Mr)

Dear Sir,
I am currently engaged in thinking about writing a book on the last days of Gorbachev, or possibly on how to convert a lawn-mower into an eye-level grill, and I should be grateful if your

readers could give me any helpful information. Should I be thinking about the paper first, eg lined or plain, or would it be better to think about moving my desk nearer the window? There is also the question of thinking about how to walk round while you're thinking about whether to move the desk or not: should you think about walking round clockwise or anti-clockwise?

Yours faithfully,
Lady Antonia Hussein

Dear Sir,
Could you settle an argument? I recently went with my friend on a How Many Words Can You Find In Stabilization? holiday to Blackburn. We had a week at the Elite Boarding House, staying in our room and trying to see how many words we could make. I got to 147 and my friend got to 148, but he said there was a word *slib*, and I said there wasn't. Then I killed him with a piece of grate. Which of us was correct?

Yours etc
568437 Wilkins, F

Household Hints: 14

A generous application of neat gin can work wonders on a dirty old hat! Go down to the pub in the dirty old hat, drink the gin, and you will find when you get home again that you cannot remember where you left the dirty old hat.

Gardener's Corner

Now that the days are getting longer, one of the really rewarding tasks is to wander out to the sunniest spot in the garden, sit down,

Collecting:
16: Victorian roll-top desks

For me, one of the most exciting discoveries in recent years came, quite by chance, when I found myself with a month or two of unexpected spare time, having finished my *List Of All The Left-handed People I Know* earlier than I had anticipated, but being not yet ready to begin work on making sure all the screws in the house were tight.

What happened was that I decided to open a drawer in my Victorian roll-top desk to measure it for an article I am preparing on *The Width Of Drawers In My House*: imagine my delight when I discovered it to be full of the most wonderful collection of items I had shoved into it over the years! Two-pin plugs from the house we used to have in Thornton Heath, a half-tube of 1963 Polos (several in mint condition), two flea-collars belonging to our cat Osric (d. 1971, see my article in our Spring Number, *Digging Up A Rockery To See If You Can Find Any Of Your Dead Cat*), nine gift diaries (1959–67) from Nardley Roofing Ltd, 136 keys to locks that we'd replaced, half a nail-scissor, 61 recipes from the *News Chronicle*, a child's sock, seven incomplete sets of playing cards, an egg-timer from Clacton (no sand), an I-Spy badge plus identification book of German bombers, 13 corks, part of a Boxing Day cigar (possibly 1972), and some two dozen less important items.

What a find! Simply washing, drying, dusting and polishing them got me from breakfast to sundown, while arranging them into little piles took me right through to midnight! Do, for example, nine dried-up ballpoints go into the same pile as the corks, or would they be more suitable among the obsolete plugs we brought from Thornton Heath? A tricky one, collectors! And at the time of going to press, I was still working out the best order for putting them all back in the drawer.

Next Week. Grading and Sorting Pocket Fluff.

and fill up all the o's and p's in your *Sunday Express*.

Personally, I like to fill up the o's with green and the p's with red, taking great care not to spread the colour outside the letter, but some keen gardeners do, I know, like to do it the other way round, and even fill up the little bit at the top of the e's in orange, though this is a much trickier job and must be undertaken with great care.

If you have any time left over, one fun job is to put moustaches on any photographs you find of Princess Diana. Also, why not try putting spectacles on all the other faces? Indeed, these can be embellished by drawing in little pupils to give the effect of a squint.

Now fold your *Sunday Express* into a hat, lean over the fence, and see the effect on your neighbour! If he says: 'Good God, isn't that Princess Diana squinting over her moustache?' a fascinating conversation may well ensue, which could get rid of most of Sunday.

Next week: Watching A Sundial

Money Down the Drain

You will have spotted that Columbia Pictures has not only shelled out one million dollars for the script of a Channel Tunnel disaster movie but has also signed up Jodie Foster to star in it, and you will therefore now be wondering exactly what it can be about this production that commands so intriguing a combination of finance and casting.

The film is in fact a sequel to Miss Foster's last great triumph, *The Silence of the Lambs*, and even more horrible. Its ghastly focus is the crazed Hannibal MacGregor, a serial Minister of Transport whose nickname was earned with his original mad plan to carry trains across the English Channel by elephant, given up only because it was not costly enough to satisfy his ghastly appetites.

He has thus replaced it with an even more diabolical one to dig a huge hole under the sea for billions of pounds he himself does not possess, but knows how to get his hands on, thanks to a silver-tongued henchman trained to persuade old ladies not only that the moon is made of green cheese, but also that he has a warehouse full of it which he is prepared to knock out at only £500 a kilo.

While it would, of course, be unfair to future filmgoers to reveal the plot, I cannot resist recommending just one or two of the set pieces you must be sure to look out for, such as the astonishing moment when Charlton Heston, playing Wilderness Secretary Moses Howard, parts Kent down the middle, swallowing up its loveliest bits, the terrifying finale in which millions of shrieking shareholders find themselves in over their heads and utterly unable to escape, and, of course, the poignant denouement when the ravishing Raine Spencer – played by Jodie Foster, whose make-up takes three days to trowel on – discovers that because the opening of the Channel Tunnel is yet again delayed, she cannot cross to France to marry Count Jean-François de Chambrun (Jeremy Paxman) and has to find a husband in Folkestone.

Horribiliser and Horribiliser

Forced not only to find the wherewithal for her income tax but also to throw one of her lovely homes open to the public in order to pay for the damage to one of the other ones, Her Majesty the Queen, we are now appalled to learn, can afford only one pair of spectacles.

Or perhaps I should say: you are now appalled to learn.

I myself have known about this truly pitiful state of affairs for some time, but have kept silent out of loyal devotion. I knew, for example, that when, just a week or so ago, the Queen was unable to find her glasses on the shelf in the Buckingham Palace boiler-room where she fully believed she had left them, she suddenly remembered putting them down on the draining-board at Balmoral, whither she was immediately chauffeured, only to have it occur to her, as the motorcade crossed the Scottish border, that she had actually slipped them into the pocket of an anorak hanging behind the door of the Sandringham outhouse where she had been worming the cat.

The moment the Queen's Flight touched down in Norfolk, however, it finally dawned on her that she had in fact last worn her glasses at Windsor Castle, when reading *Sporting Life* in the bath.

How, you will be asking, can I possibly be in a position to know all this? The truth is that I have an authoritative contact ensconced deep within the M15 Royal Shouting Match Bugging Department, who has sent me a full transcript of HRH Prince Philip's reactions to his poor wife's misfortunes.

However, much as I should like to publish these fascinating observations in the national interest, they are all, I'm sorry to say, unprintable.

Only Half a Crown

National rejoicing at Her Majesty's gracious decision to take a few quid off her subjects by throwing Buck House open to them was followed last week, as you will have read, by both public and parliamentary clamour for her to do the same with the royal yacht *Britannia*.

Now, while she let it be known that she was not yet ready to profit from such demands, these did, however, set the sovereign thinking, according to authoritative sources close to her accountant.

Quite soon now, as I understand it, anyone wishing to be driven around waving and smiling will be able to hire coaches for £50 an hour per head (not more than 14 people per coach, no singing, and please state whether open, closed, glass, or golden with your order), while individual horses will be available for rent at the same rate from the Royal Mews by any member of the public with a colour to troop (regiment not provided).

It may also be possible, for a commensurate surcharge, to have yourself attended by footmen, ushers, butlers, ladies-in-waiting, or pages, always provided these do not have prior commitments at weddings, barmitzvahs, barbecues, stag nights, Windsorgrams, and so forth, while, for the less well-heeled, a wide range of corgis will be on offer for walkies at £3 an hour (with, of course, generous discounts for OAPs and the unwaged). However, rumours that an 0898 number is to be provided for anyone wishing to chat intimately with Prince Charles's geraniums are, at the time of going to press, sadly unfounded.

A Yeti Writes . . .

Dear Sir,

It is a right dog's dinner up here, and I speak as one who knows, I have just this minute trodden in a basinful of half-eaten marrowbone jelly, the only blessing is I have not trodden in anything worse, no thanks to the Cornhill & Hedges First Dog Up Everest Expedition.

It is bad enough being kept awake all night by the Virgin Natwest Chicken MacNugget Ensemble rehearsing the repertoire they intend to play as soon as they become the first string quartet to reach the summit, without having a ropeful of canine mountaineers widdling on you. You would not believe the current state of Everest (unless, of course, you have been a lucky winner of the WH Rumbelow Gold Blend Glorious Weekend Up Everest For Two contest).

Take yesterday: I had just got back from watching the Castlemaine Marlboro Welshwomen's Zimmer Frame assault on the North Col and was stuck at the Khumbu Glacier traffic lights patiently waiting for the Basingstoke Young Conservatives Formation Dancers to pass by on their party-fundraising foxtrot up the South Face, when a woman in the queue behind poked my hump with her umbrella and shouted, 'Oy, Sambo, is this the way to the Himalaya Tesco's?' I pointed to a line of rusting trolleys dumped along the West Cwym, and her husband said, 'Hasn't he got a tongue in his head? If they can't speak English why the hell do they come over here?'

I cannot take much more of this. I am supposed to be a spine-chilling legend, I am supposed to be an insoluble enigma, I am supposed to inspire fear, all you are supposed to see of me is a giant footprint in the eternal wossname, but how can I do my job, now? My job is to be abominable, but when it comes to what's abominable these days, I am not even in the bloody frame.

Yours etc

Thought for Today

I have discovered that Miss Joan Collins, who this morning receives her free bus pass, was blowing out the candle on her first birthday cake on the day that Bonnie and Clyde were shot. There is a bottle of champagne awaiting any reader who knows anything more interesting than that about 23 May 1934.

Something for the Weekend

Like me, you must have been hugely encouraged by last week's joint decision on the part of President and Mrs Clinton to have their hair cut.

Not surprisingly, the move and its consequences occupied international front pages for several days, since the world, while recognizing Bill Clinton to have been a great candidate, had been waiting for six months to discover whether he was also a great president.

Nor need I remind you that there were also grave fears on the part of sceptics that the First Lady might have been exercising undue influence over him.

Not so. While the radiant Hillary opted for a major cut which tacitly (but shrewdly) acknowledged the fact that she was not so significant that the world could be shaken by so radical a step on her part, the President did no more than ask for a little bit off the sides, leave the top full, and no greasy stuff. Bill Clinton is unquestionably his own man, and, God be praised, ours too.

It couldn't have been an easy decision to make, but he made it. This is not the end. It is not even the beginning of the end. But it is, perhaps, the end of the beginning.

A Matter of Priorities

Though unwilling to chuck in my lot with those who believe John Major to be incapable of giving a straight answer to a straight question, I have to confess to a certain nagging unease at his snappy Commons reply to Opposition demands for assurances on the future of the welfare state.

Chief Secretary Michael Portillo, retorted the Prime Minister, would be examining all aspects of the matter, 'and he knows that in doing so he must protect the position of the most vulnerable members of society'. As I am not entirely confident of decoding this unequivocally, I shall just have to give him the benefit of the doubt and trust that this was something more than a reference to the Conservative Government.

A Rabbit Writes . . .

Dear Sir,

May I crave the indulgence of your esteemed columns to intervene in the current dispute between British Rail and the nation's farmers over the proposed ethnic cleansing of my people?

I have a solution which should be not only acceptable to both sides, but also beneficial to the entire population, rabbit and human alike. As you know, the row concerns the proliferation of the rabbit community on railway embankments and the consequence that once they have proliferated. they proceed to eat their way through surrounding crops like nobody's business. The NFU therefore not only want damages, they want BR to exterminate us.

There is another way.

Why we are proliferating is all down to leaves on the line, frozen points, the wrong sort of drizzle, staff cuts, cock-eyed management, antique rolling stock, John MacGregor, Bob Reid, Jimmy Knapp, ie the utter collapse of the rail system. In the old days, no rabbit in its right mind would choose an embankment for a bit of how's your father, trains belting by every two minutes, noise, vibration, people staring, not to mention slipstream likely to blow loved ones all over the shop at critical moments, it is not exactly candle-lit dinner and Nat King Cole. Whereas today you hardly see a train, and when you do it is creeping along at 2 mph, I could introduce you to rabbits who've had as many as three meaningful relationships between spotting the 8.14 from Orpington on the horizon and having it trundle alongside, if they made *Brief Encounter* now, they would have to show Trevor Howard and Celia Wossname going at it like knives, you cannot sit in a waiting-room fancying someone for nine hours, I am a rabbit and know whereof I speak. So all BR has to do to avoid the current aggro is provide a decent service. Simple, really. God knows why nobody's thought of it before.

Yours etc

Thick Blue Square

I find myself at a complete loss to understand the present bitter argument over whether policemen should be forced to declare their membership of the Freemasons. There is no conflict of interest here whatever.

And not only is the resolution as plain as the knee on your leg, it creates a golden opportunity which our haplessly crime-ridden society should on no account be allowed to miss.

Far from insisting that being a mason has nothing whatever to do with being a policeman, masons of all trades and professions should be encouraged, and as quickly as possible, to take to the highways and byways as active supporters of our undermanned and hard-pressed constabulary. There are countless thousands of these able-bodied fellows already formed into highly organized units throughout the country, and were they now to surge on to our nocturnal streets, ritual bags menacingly concealing their faces, trousers rolled up to expose their sturdy moonlit calves, baize pinnies flapping with all the blood-curdling intimidation of the toughest Highland regiments, and their fists brandishing stout staves of office and stiletto-sharp compasses, who can doubt but that those streets would instantly be rendered empty of terrified villains and safe for decent humans beings to walk?

Fatal Flaw

Since you will all be craning towards your fireside tubes tonight when Mrs Alan Clark will compare her hapless husband to a Greek tragic hero, I have been putting in a little research on all our behalves in the hope of identifying the particular tragic hero she had in mind.

I am now convinced that she must be thinking of Ludicrus, son of an oyster on whom Zeus, descending from Olympus in the guise of half a lemon, got himself squeezed. Born as a talking pearl, Ludicrus was soon attached to a golden chain and hung around the neck of the voluptuous Bimbea; to whom Ludicrus, frenzied by what he was dangling on, immediately made an improper suggestion. In consequence, the gods turned him into a pilchard. It did not help. Of the 40 female pilchards in the ornamental pond in which Ludicrus was placed, 32 had, within the week, complained that they had been the victims of a right seeing-to, while the other eight had had themselves turned into walnuts to escape his advances, a course which even then had not been entirely successful.

Ludicrus being, however, immortal, no option existed but to transmogrify him yet again in the hope of hitting on something which would keep its hands to itself. He became a tree, until a number of nesting birds began laying pilchards, and then, in rapid succession, a boot, a saucepan, a glass eye, and a pot-hole, each time managing, somehow, to overcome incredible odds in order to feed his insatiable desires. It was at this point that Ludicrus was, quite fortuitously, turned into a lyre by Terpsichore, who was reforming her backing group, whereupon his little ways led, not surprisingly, to his being described by their warm-up man, Tarbi, as the most consummate lyre anyone had ever come across. Lousy though it was, the joke gave the gods an idea. They immediately turned Ludicrus into a minor politician: a ghastly fate, perhaps, but one, as you would expect in a Greek tragedy, entirely of his own making.

Coming Events in June

JUNE 7: **Surbiton Fayre**: Sardine exhibition; knobbly head contest; mouse-juggling (Special Branch vs. Flat Earth Society Juniors); scenic walk round Tesco's; Josef Goebbels Lookalike Dinner & Dance.
JUNE 9: **Prudential World Smoking Cup**, *Cowdray Park*, in aid of hernia research.
JUNE 10: **Cockfosters Bach Festival**: 8th Tawny Pack Symphony Orchestra plays Bits of Toccata and Bear's Picnic, Concerto for Kazoo and Beer Bottles, and Noises Bach Made by Putting His Hand In His Armpit And Bringing His Arm Down.
JUNE 11: **Guy Fawkes Night Dance**, *Shamrock Ballroom, Kilburn*.
JUNE 15: **Grodzinski Puppet Theatre of Kiev** perform *Private Lives*, Crystal Palace Sports Centre (dogs not admitted).
JUNE 18: **Early Years Of Double Glazing Pageant**, *Bermondsey*. Floats, whelk tent, Red Arrows Obstetrics Team display, dog-strangling, tug o'war (Gay Rights XV vs. Ghurkas).
JUNE 21: **House of Lords Reggae Finals**, *Skirmdale*, OR **Second Test Match** (consult local paper for details).
JUNE 24: **Friends of Pope Pius XII Floral Dance**, *Golders Green Kennel Club*, and afterwards at The Gnat & Walnut, Bromley.
JUNE 27: **National Model Lesbian Exhibition**, *Olympia*.
JUNE 30: **Grand Open Air Celebrity Concert**, *Potters Bar*, with Martha Snelling, JD Breene, Eric Foskett's Dancing Turkeys, Nicholas Parsons, George McShane and Sambo, the Noles Novelty Trio, and 'Hairy'.

A Parrot Writes

Dear Sir,

As a Norwegian Blue, I have taken some stick in my time, I do not mind saying.

It is some 18 years now since I was first held up to scorn, ridicule and contempt by a certain Monty Python, who subsequently went on to make a fortune out of 1,436 repeats of what his sniggering bloody countrymen were pleased to describe as 'a classic comedy sketch', if all parrots are comic, and all dead parrots are hilarious, then dead Norwegian parrots are the funniest things in the world. Well, sunshine, every wossname has his day. I am, I think, no more vindictive than the next parrot, but I have been waiting since 1975 for revenge. And, believe me, it was worth the wait. It came with Wednesday night's England–Norway match, out of the blue, if you will forgive the pun. Even if you won't, actually, because I do not give a toss, I could not care less, it is my turn to snigger, now.

English football has passed on. It is no more. It has ceased to be. It has expired and gone to meet its maker. It is a stiff. It has curled up its tootsies, it has shuffled off this mortal coil, it has rung down the curtain and joined the bleeding choir invisible. All statements to the effect that English football is still a going concern are now inoperable.

THIS IS AN EX-GAME!

No doubt Mr Graham Taylor and his gang of clapped-out dead-beats have been going around claiming they are sick as parrots. Well, that is just one more thing they do not have the first idea about. There is nothing sick about parrots. We are over the moon. As we say up Norway, satire is a game of two halves.

Yours etc

Mind How You Grow!

Much as we all applaud the police for this week's apparently brilliant solution to the escalating burglary threat, householders should be advised that growing a hedge round their property to keep criminals out is fraught with problems.

They have not, I fear, been adequately apprised.

While it may seem simple enough, if you wake in the middle of the night to a suspicious footfall and a glimpse through the curtains of a man in a striped jersey, to run downstairs with a packet of seeds in order to sow, say, a sturdy pyrancantha thicket between chummy and your premises, remember that the citizen is entitled to use only reasonable force to protect his property.

He may not punish. He may not take the law into his own hands. His hedge is a defence, not a weapon.

Should, for example, your vegetation infect any would-be intruder with black spot, mildew, scab, or similar, you could well find that it is you, not he, who is facing prosecution. Should he, on returning home, discover that his clothes have become infested with greenfly, red spider mites, leafhoppers, and so forth, he would be completely within his rights to have you arrested as a vigilante and sent down for five years. If, furthermore, as the result of contact with your foliage, he develops wilt or curl, you may also be liable to a civil suit brought by his wife.

I raised these points with the Serious Shrubs Squad, and they have reluctantly confirmed that it is incumbent upon the householder to ensure that all hedges are non-aggressive, to which end they must be regularly sprayed and otherwise treated against disease and dangerous insects. But be warned that even this can pose problems: should a burglar find, as the result of pesticidal chemicals, that his eyes are watering on the bus home, or that he has to ask the driver to stop so that he can vomit or, at the very least, have a good scratch, you could be looking at a heavy fine, or imprisonment, or — if, say, he cannot stop sneezing — both.

Gypsy Rose Coren's Stars for '94

Aries

A slightly unsettling year. You will be lucky in guttering, but get a verruca. An uncle you have not seen for many years will be assaulted by warders. In June, a parcel from Samoa will turn out to be for the people next door, and in July a German will ask you to explain cricket. During a cheap autumn break in Paignton, a dead hake will wash up on your shoe, and an olive in your nostril will have to be removed under anaesthetic, but in November you will receive quite good news about a loved shirt. At work, your door will stick. During the Christmas festivities, an uncle will pass a kidney stone. Lucky furniture: sideboard.

Taurus

For Taureans, 1994 is packed with favourable auguries! On 16 February, the thing on the cat's ear will shrivel, and around mid-April you will find a short cut to Sainsbury's. A fence leads to romance during the late summer, but beware of an old docker carrying pencils; he bodes ill. In autumn, a clash with royalty will end happily, and at work a colleague given to sneering at your Anglepoise lamp will fall down a lift-shaft. October, mind, will bring news of an unfathomable insect pregnancy, and an old friend will mistake you for Desmond Wilcox, but in December you will be given a very useful cardboard box. Lucky cutlery: fork.

Gemini

Not, I'm afraid, the happiest of years. An unexpected trip across water will lead to alopecia, a loved one will become increasingly left-handed, your watch will turn out to be unfashionable, and, in late spring, you will discover that the postal origami course you have been following all winter was being conducted by an imposter. Things perk up in June, however, when a bottle of Tia Maria won in a Gas Board raffle will prove to be corked, and you will receive £8.95 in lieu; but in July your number-plate will drop off. By December, though, you will feel confident enough to advertise your wig in the local paper. Unlucky salad: prawn.

Cancer

A fascinating year in some respects, though not without its pitfalls. A grave tennis accident will prove the honesty of an earlier spouse, but the conjunction of Neptune with Orion in June could mean a long journey to either Rhyl or Macclesfield and a great deal of unsavoury paperwork at the end. Winter brings a sudden flurry of activity with (a) distant relatives trying to persuade you to invest in a cello, (b) a save-the-gibbon walk going badly wrong, and (c) a busker offering to exchange his cap for your sandwiches.

Leo

Lionfolk will experience a somewhat puzzling twelvemonth. Soon after New Year's Day, a brass band will appear on your doorstep seeking funds for a tunnel linking Madagascar to the mainland. In March, you will become convinced that *The Sound of Music* may be open to a lubricious interpretation, but by Midsummer's Day this will have yielded to a preoccupation with canasta. October, with Mars in the House of Fraser, is a dire month: your teeth will smart, and a nit will appear on a loved one. In November, however, you will receive an uplift from a sailor.

Virgo

An excellent year! All the problems of 1993 will disappear, although phantom pains from the hammer toe may persist until Martinmas. In April, a team of schoolgirl cricketers bound for a tour of the Cinque Ports will pose for Polaroid snapshots and stay to rod out the drains, and on Easter Monday, a mynah bird left in your care by a deserter will be invited on to **Start the Week***. Celebrities abound: a postcard from a Clacton friend will bring news that he has successfully insulted Angela Rippon, and, in October, you will see Jimmy Young from the top of a bus.*

Libra

In January, with Saturn at +0.8 magnitude in the constellation of Libra, you would be well-advised to keep away from copper piping, mice, gin, walnuts, foothills, old Lita Rosa 78s, hydrometers, poetry, Estonians, and anything resembling anthracite or wrens. By March, when your lucky tune is *Shagpone Louie Done Got Mah*

*Foot***, things will begin to look up, but watch out in April for an ex-IRA brigadier who will come to your door and attempt to buy your double-glazing. In June, a neighbour who has confused Sunbeam-Talbot with Armstrong-Siddeley may turn nasty.**

Scorpio

As Pluto comes under the influence of Betelgeuse, Scorpians may find it difficult to park. However, a red-headed man from across the seas will arrive with exciting news of Barry Manilow leisurewear. Love-interest is strongest around July, and some of you may have to be roped to a gatepost until Venus has entered her third phase. Do not despair: a gentle aura surrounding All Hallows' Eve indicates this would be a good time to sell up low-coupon gilts and run away to Maracaibo with a big mulatto stripper. Lucky cattle: ox. Unlucky software: MacBeth.

Sagittarius

Sagittarians are, I fear, in for a somewhat distressing 1994. In January a kilt will

unravel publicly, causing behaviour likely to lead to a breach of the peace, and in mid-February a tarantula lurking in a hand of Tobago bananas will prove to be worth less than 50p. In April, a Cypriot tax-collector will finally lose patience with your snide remarks and ship your sister to the Famagusta Working Men's Club under a three-year contract requiring her to dance with a gherkin, and on a September fishing weekend in Skelmersdale, a friend's dog will lick out your contact lens.

Capricorn

After the unprecedented disasters of 1993, those of you born under the goat will enjoy stunning good fortune throughout the coming year! Rust in your lorry will respond to astral massage, your spastic colon will find a tenacious adversary in Joan the Wad, the pervert in the upstairs maisonette will receive a splinter from his knothole and lose the sight of his left eye, and the moth in your herringbone overcoat will figure prominently in *Wildlife on One***. In June, height regulations will be waived to allow you to join the Metropolitan Water Board Ukulele Band.**

Aquarius

Water-carriers would be well-advised to tread with care throughout the coming year, above all avoiding distillers,

members of the Planning Bar, lower-order batsmen, pursers, boilermakers, cross-dressers, and Colonel Gaddafi. In March, fluency in Flemish will prove useless, and sometime in June a misplaced shoehorn will result in a brief spell in Broadmoor; things improve slightly in August, when a black man will bring news of a breakthrough in marine engineering, but at the end of October a bout of accidental adultery could well result in demotion.

Pisces

Pisceans will experience a fairly calm year, though a loose roof-tile in May will act as a salutary reminder that Orion is on an elliptical orbit through the miasma of Sirius. However, the surgeon will tell you an Irish joke you have heard only twice before. In July, a free lunch at Bellevue Zoo will end in tears, but later a Welshwoman with a wall-eye will bring good tidings of a mislaid sink, and in autumn a surprise windfall will enable you to buy **The Sir Geoffrey Howe Cookbook***. A funny look from a friend's horse could mar Christmas. Lucky tit: blue.*

Horses for Courses

President Niyazov of Turkmenistan, you will have read, is deeply upset that the thoroughbred stallion he gave to John Major for his 50th birthday on 29 March has still not been collected. He finds himself, it seems, at an utter loss to understand the Prime Minister's inaction.

Clearly, Mr Niyazov is a stranger to the Downing Street process. The truth about his gift horse is that for some months past, the Cabinet has occupied itself with little else. Originally it decided, since the transportation involved huge foreign expenditure, that this was a Treasury remit.

Mr Lamont immediately issued a press release stating that, as Britain was, and would forever remain, a member of the Exchange Horse Mechanism, by which our horses were allowed to float against a basket of European ones, the cost would be covered under an EC set-aside on which payment would not fall due until 1998. The next day, unfortunately, he found himself compelled to take Britain out of the EHM for personal reasons rumoured to involve a woman in his basement who had been using a saddle and riding-crop for unlicensed profit. But he had, he insisted, no regrets about the horse, and sang 'A four-legged friend, a four-legged friend, he'll never let you down,' in Newbury, to prove it.

The buck then passed to Mr John Patten, who said that the horse would be given a visa as soon as it had sat certain tests. He did not know what form these tests would take, so he had consulted experts on horse-testing, all of whom said tests would do incalculable harm to the horse, never mind all the bloody paperwork, so on the basis of this advice, Mr Patten naturally concluded that the experts were off their heads. He insisted that the horse would be tested before breakfast, before lunch, and before dinner, whereupon Mr Michael Heseltine screamed that that was a Board of Trade matter, and if it was going to be done properly, then all the stables in Britain would have to be shut down, and then opened again, and then shut down again, until horses saw reason.

The only way the PM could settle this row was to kick the ball into the Home Secretary's court. Mr Clarke's Horse Justice Act was then rushed in, but when it transpired that because President Niyazov's weekly disposable income exceeded £100 he would, under the unit system, have to pay some £984,000 in export duty, it was rushed out again, leaving Mr Major nowhere to turn but to Virginia Bottomley. Her reaction was to write to the President saying that he should not assume that because his gift was a three-year-old, it counted as an infant; in horse terms, it was an adult and if it required dentures or spectacles, it would have to pay for them itself.

At this, Turkmenistan threatened to break off diplomatic relations with Britain unless the Cabinet was reshuffled. This was, of course, done, but to little effect. At the time of going to press, however, it is hoped that the new Cabinet may accept Mr Douglas Hurd's advice to consider the Vance–Owen compromise on Turkmenistan.

This requires Mr Michael Mates to arrange to have the horse engraved and sent to Mr Asil Nadir, who would pick up all the transportation costs in return for a free pardon and a knighthood.

No Peace for the Wicked

I do hope you'll forgive my appearing to bang on about religion, but this is, after all, the sabbath day, and thus no bad time to express grave doubts concerning the Automatic Confession Machine, whose invention by Professor Gregory Garvey of Concordia University, Montreal, was gleefully announced last Thursday. In an article in the *New Scientist*, Prof Garvey explained how the device worked: the guilty type in their sins on a computer keyboard, whereupon they receive an instant print-out of the penance required, in the form of Hail Marys and Our Fathers. What he did not of course explain was how the device might *fail* to work, because you and I know that divine infallibility does not extend to computers. I therefore strongly advise any of my readers who may have slipped from the straight and narrow not to touch this thing's keyboard with a bargepole: wicked though it may be to, for example, covet one's neighbour's ox, it hardly deserves a gas bill for £18,098,326.97, a daily delivery of cedarwood room extensions, an urgent request from Virginia Bottomley to come in and have your hernia seen to right away or miss your place in the queue until 1998, a dawn raid by the West Midlands constabulary acting on information received that you committed an act of gross public indecency at a recent Kegworth boot sale, or, worst of all, a lifetime's subscription to *Reader's Digest*.